OLD TESTAMENT DAYS

An Activity Guide

NANCY I. SANDERS

CHICAGO
REVIEW
PRESS

D1611316

Library of Congress Cataloging-in-Publication Data

Sanders, Nancy I.
    Old Testament days : an activity guide / Nancy I. Sanders.
    p.   cm.
    Includes bibliographical references.
    Summary: Uses more than eighty activities and projects to provide insight
into life in the Middle East during the period covered by the Old Testament
    ISBN 1-55652-354-8
    1. Bible. O.T.—Antiquities Juvenile literature. 2. Palestine—
Social life and customs Juvenile literature. [1. Bible. O.T.—
Antiquities 2. Middle East—Civilizations—To 622.] I. Title.
BS621.S265   1999
372.89´044—dc21

99-12454
CIP

The author and the publisher disclaim all liability for use of the information contained
in this book.

Cover design and illustrations: Fran Lee
Interior design and illustration: Rattray Design

©1999 by Nancy L. Sanders
All rights reserved
First edition
Published by Chicago Review Press, Incorporated
814 North Franklin Street
Chicago, Illinois 60610
ISBN 1-55652-354-8
Printed in the United States of America
5 4 3 2 1

THIS BOOK IS dedicated to Becky Calhoun. Your bright smile and joyful outlook make you a beautiful ray of sunshine in people's lives. Thanks for the special memories you've brought to me and my family through the photograph you took of Grandpa.

CONTENTS

ACKNOWLEDGMENTS

THANK YOU Dan and Ben for all your help making the craft samples for this book and for letting me borrow your creative ideas!

Thanks to Stephanie Seipp for testing this book with your home-schooling friends. You're still a wonderful neighbor even though you've moved across town. Thanks to the different linguists, especially Steven Schaufele of Soochow University in Taiwan, for helping me gain a better understanding of Hebrew numbers. Thank you Cynthia Sherry for helping make this dream a reality.

TIME LINE

Living in Tents

2090 B.C.*
Abraham leaves Ur.

1970 B.C.
Isaac is born to Abraham and Sarah.

1920 B.C.
Jacob marries and has many children.

1875 B.C.
Jacob's family moves to Egypt.

1700 B.C.
The Israelites are slaves in Egypt.

Into Egypt and Out Again

1446 B.C.
Moses leads the Israelites out of Egypt.

Prophets and Kings

960 B.C.
Solomon builds the Temple.

1011 B.C.
David becomes king.

1400 B.C.
Israelites enter the Promised Land.

1445 B.C.
Moses receives the Ten Commandments.

605 B.C.
Jerusalem is captured and captives are taken away.

Back to the City

Far Away from Home

586 B.C.
Jerusalem, the Temple, and the city walls are destroyed.

538 B.C.
The first group of Jews returns to Jerusalem.

516 B.C.
The second Temple is built.

445 B.C.
Nehemiah finishes rebuilding the wall around the city of Jerusalem.

430 B.C.
The last book of the Old Testament is written.

* All dates are approximate.

INTRODUCTION

When you're thirsty, you grab a drink of water from the kitchen sink. But how did thirsty kids get a drink two to four thousand years ago, when the Old Testament was being written? When you settle in bed to read your favorite mystery, you turn on the light. But how did kids see in the dark when they lived so long ago that most people didn't even build houses? And next time you shop until you drop at the coolest store in the mall, just think of it! Kids living during Old Testament days helped make their own clothes by chasing down the family sheep and cutting the wool off their baa-aa-aacks!

How do we know what people did who lived so long ago? There aren't eyewitnesses to tell us what they saw. There are, however, a lot of clues that leave trails for us to follow. Special scientists called *archaeologists* (say it: ark-ee-ALL-uh-gists)

follow these trails of clues to dig up treasures that help answer our questions. There are also plenty of clues found in the Old Testament itself.

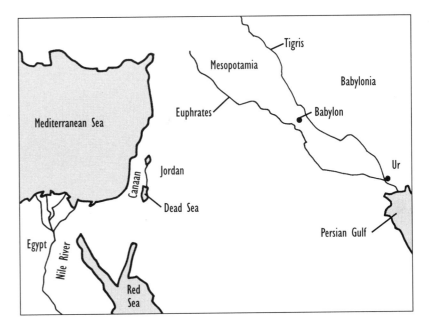

4,000 years ago

1

The Old Testament talks about key people who lived long ago in and around the area we know as the Middle East. Today, we find countries in this area such as Kuwait, Jordan, Syria, Lebanon, Israel, Iraq, Egypt, Iran, and Saudi Arabia. But four thousand years ago, most of the land was a dry wilderness. Large cities in Babylonia and Egypt thrived near rivers like the Nile, the Tigris, and the Euphrates, but with harsh desert conditions, only small communities with their local kings existed far from these rivers.

DIG YOUR OWN ARCHAEOLOGICAL SITE

When archaeologists search for clues about people who lived during Old Testament days, they take a step-by-step approach. Their careful methods make sure that everything they find can be pieced together to paint a colorful picture of the past.

Step 1 Archaeologists get a license that gives them permission to explore a certain area or site.

Step 2 The archaeologists map out the site and divide the area into equal squares. These squares are called a site grid.

Step 3 They use shovels to dig away the dirt and grass from the top of the area.

Step 4 Using small hand shovels, archaeologists dig slowly and carefully down through the dirt. Videos, photographs, and careful notes are taken in order to keep a record of everything that's found.

Step 5 Fine screens are used to sift dirt so that even the smallest items are found. Everything that is dug up is put into separate bags and sent to a laboratory.

Step 6 When the search is over, archaeologists carefully put the dirt back into the holes they dug up so that the area looks the way it did before they arrived.

Step 7 At the laboratory, archaeologists look at

all the items they found. They put broken pieces back together and look for clues about people who lived during Old Testament days. Then they write reports to tell us what they found.

You can dig your own archaeological site.

Materials

Small clay pot

Acrylic craft paints

Paintbrush

Small hammer

Sandbox

Hand shovel

Bag

Paper

Pencil

Glue

Purchase a small clay pot, the kind you plant flowers in. Use acrylic craft paints to paint simple designs on your pot. You can even use the hieroglyphs found on page 7 to paint a secret message.

This pot says "days long ago."

Take your pot outside and put it on the ground. Hit the pot once with a small hammer, breaking it into pieces. Try not to break it into too many small

pieces. Then ask a friend to bury the pieces in a small area of a sandbox.

Use a hand shovel to dig for your pot. Store the pieces in a bag. When you think you've found all the pieces, draw a small picture of each piece and label it with a number.

Now try gluing all the pieces back together. If some of the pieces are missing, revisit the sandbox and continue digging. After the pot is glued back together, display it in your room as one of your important treasures.

KEYS TO UNLOCK THE PAST

Over the years, as people looked for clues about life during Old Testament days, they made many important discoveries. Two of the most important discoveries were the Rosetta stone and the Dead Sea scrolls. (Say it: skrolls.)

A *scroll* is a type of book that is rolled up in one long page. The Dead Sea scrolls are very, very old. Many of them are more than 2,000 old!

The story of how these ancient scrolls were discovered has varied, but one story is that the first scrolls were found by a shepherd boy. His goat ran away from him and jumped into a cave. The shepherd boy threw a stone into the cave and heard clay pots breaking. He called his friend, and the two boys climbed into the cave. They found clay jars inside the cave. Sticking out from the tops of the jars were the scrolls.

Since then, many scrolls have been found in the caves around the Dead Sea. It's possible that a Jewish sect called the Essenes placed them there. These scrolls contain the books of the Old Testament. They also contain other books that tell us many details about life during Old Testament days.

In 1798, the French general Napoleon and his officers visited Egypt to study its ancient past. During their trip, they found the Rosetta stone. (Say it: rose-ETTA.) The message on the Rosetta stone was written three times in three different languages and told about an important ruler. One of the languages was Greek, one was demotic script, and one was Egyptian hieroglyphs. This stone helped early archaeologists read and interpret hieroglyphs. We were finally able to read the carvings made in ancient Egypt. Since Egypt was such an important country during the time that the Old Testament was written, understanding hieroglyphs helped us discover many important details about life during Old Testament times.

Here's the alphabet using hieroglyphs. Try writing your name using these pictures. Write a message to a friend using hieroglyphs.

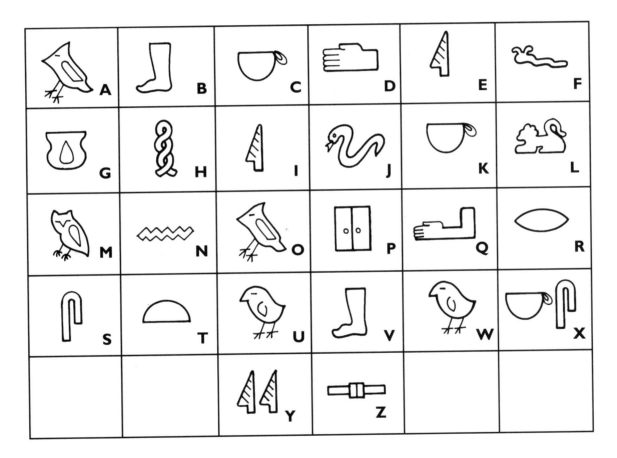

Some letters use the same symbol, such as _u_ and _w_. Can you find the others?

LIVING IN TENTS

Growing Up in Ur

In Babylonia, there was an important city named Ur. (Say it: it rhymes with fur.) The city of Ur reached its glory around the year 2090 B.C. In the rich soil around Ur, farmers grew huge crops of grains, beans, olives, and grapes in order to feed the large number of people living in the city. Artists and craftspeople who lived in Ur made beautiful jewelry. They designed instruments, crowns, and helmets and decorated them with gold. Merchants traveled to Ur to trade their cargo with the people living there.

Cities in those days were surrounded by a protective wall. The houses were built inside the wall. The people in Ur made their houses from mud bricks. The houses were small compared to ours and were often built very close together. In the middle of the crowded city of Ur stood the temple buildings. A tall tower was built at the temple. This tower was called a *ziggurat*, which means "holy mountain." (Say it: ZIG-er-at.)

It was in this exciting city that two important people from the Old Testament were born. Abraham and Sarah were born in Ur and grew up there. As children, they probably visited the crowded markets, where they heard goats bleating and smelled beans cooking. Abraham and Sarah probably walked past the ziggurat hundreds of times as they visited relatives who lived in other parts of the city. Many of their friends went to school in Ur, where they studied subjects such as math, geography, and writing. Children in Ur learned how to write on clay tablets using a special stick the size of a pencil.

A ZIGGURAT

The ziggurat in Ur was a remarkable building several stories high. The temple priests walked up long rows of stairs to get from one story to the next.

Materials

Empty rectangular cracker or cereal boxes of a variety of sizes

Glue

Paintbrush

Craft or tempera paint, brown

Measuring spoons

Cornmeal

Measuring cups

Permanent marker

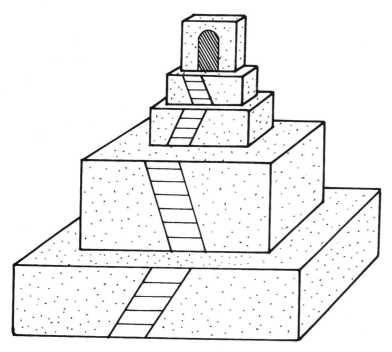

a ziggurat

Stack the boxes with the largest box on the bottom and the smallest one on top. Glue the boxes together. Paint the boxes brown. When the first coat of paint is dry, paint a second time with a mixture of 1 tablespoon of cornmeal to $\frac{1}{8}$ cup of paint. This paint mixture will give texture to the sides of the ziggurat. When the paint is dry, use a permanent marker to draw long rows of stairs up the side. Draw a door in the top level.

Abraham and His Family Leave Ur

Abraham and Sarah eventually married. One day God told Abraham to pack up his belongings and move away from Ur and he would lead Abraham and his family to a new place to live. A lot of people move to a new city today, but back in Old Testament days, this was a very difficult thing to do. Abraham and Sarah were leaving their mud-brick house in a prosperous city and heading out into the wilderness and the desert, where they would have to live in tents.

But Abraham and Sarah believed that this was what God wanted them to do, so they packed everything they owned and headed out of town. Some of their relatives went with them. Many years after leaving Ur, Abraham and Sarah had a son and named him Isaac. For the rest of their lives, Abraham, Sarah, and Isaac traveled around. Wherever they settled, they lived in tents.

TRAVELING FROM PLACE TO PLACE

Abraham and his family traveled throughout the countryside, living in places where they found grass and water for their flocks of sheep and goats. Since they moved around a lot, they needed to carry their "house" with them, which is why they lived in tents. People who live in tents are called *nomads*. (Say it: NO-mads.) Donkeys carried their possessions from place to place, so their home and everything in it had to be folded and packed.

Abraham and Sarah were very wealthy. They kept a lot of animals and hired a lot of servants. They needed a lot of tents to provide shelter for everyone. The servants and their children worked hard to pack Abraham and Sarah's belongings when they left an area and they worked hard to set everything up when they arrived at a new place.

Water wasn't plentiful since most of the countryside was hot and dry. Abraham and his family traveled from one source of water to the next. Sometimes they found small rivers, but mostly they stopped at wells dug deep into the dry ground. Wherever they went, they always looked for places with enough food to feed all the flocks, their family, and the large number of servants.

A SLEEPING MAT

Not only did Abraham and his family carry their tents with them, but they also carried their beds. Their beds weren't made of big, stiff mattresses like ours. Their beds were soft mats stuffed with wool from their sheep. These mats were easy to roll up and pack when it was time to move to a new water hole.

Find two towels that you fit on when you lie down. Spread a thin layer of fiberfill on top of one of the towels, staying away from the edge. Spread glue around the edges of this towel. Place the second towel carefully over the first and firmly press the edges together. Allow the glue to dry completely before using your sleeping mat. You can roll up your soft bed when you're not using it and unroll it when you need a place to rest.

Materials

2 large towels, same size

Polyester fiberfill
(available in fabric stores)

Fabric glue

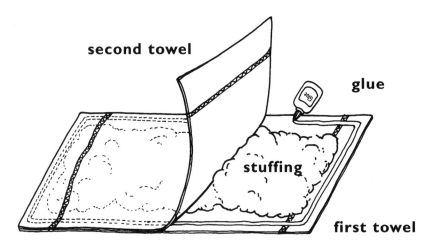

second towel

glue

stuffing

first towel

A PICNIC EVERY DAY

Even the table had to be packed up and carried along, so it was made from leather. Abraham's servants spread the table out on the ground. The leather was shaped like a circle, and everyone ate while sitting around it on the ground. Every meal for Abraham and his family looked just like a picnic for your family today!

The leather table had loops attached all around the edge of it. Each time Abraham's family moved, they threaded a rope through all the loops. Pulling the rope tight, the table formed a bag the travelers used to carry their possessions in.

Make a Table

Here's how to make a table like the one Abraham, Sarah, and Isaac used.

Materials

Small round fabric tablecloth or piece of knit fabric cut into a 2- to 3-foot-wide circle

Pencil

Ruler

Scissors

2 yards 1-inch-wide fabric ribbon

Lay the fabric on a flat surface. Draw a one-inch slit every two to three inches all the way around the outer edge of the fabric. Cut the slits. Make an even number of slits, trying to space them evenly along the edge.

To use the table, spread it out flat on the floor and put all your food on it. Enjoy a picnic. When you are finished eating, put the food away, wash your

A table could be formed into a bag.

plastic dishes, and place your clean dishes in the middle of the table. Thread the ribbon through the fabric slits in an over-under pattern. Knot the ends of the ribbon so it won't unthread. Then bring the table edges together by carefully pulling the ribbon. Now you have a bag for carrying your dishes!

Lentil Stew

Abraham and his family ate different kinds of food from what we're used to eating. They didn't buy their food in stores. They had to eat food from animals they raised and from the plants that grew in the area. A typical meal they might have eaten included a stew made from lentils, cheese made from goat's milk, and dried figs.

To host your own Old Testament days picnic, look for goat's cheese and dried figs in a specialty section of your grocery store. Here's a recipe for a lentil stew that you might enjoy.

4 one-cup servings

Ingredients

$^3/_4$ cup lentils, any variety

$^1/_4$ cup brown rice

$3^1/_2$ cups water

1 cup grated cheddar cheese

Salt to taste

Whole wheat tortillas

Utensils

Measuring cup

Strainer

Pot with lid

Large spoon

Bowls

(Adult help suggested.)

Place the lentils in a strainer or bowl and check for and remove any small pebbles. Rinse the lentils and rice. Combine lentils, rice, and water in a pot. Bring to a boil. Cover and simmer for 40 minutes or until the water is absorbed. Stir in the cheese and salt.

Serve the lentil stew in bowls. To eat, tear off a two-inch piece of tortilla. Scoop some stew up in the tortilla and take a bite, tortilla and all! In the desert, people ate bread that was round and flat but often more crispy than a soft tortilla.

People who lived in the desert used bread to scoop up stew.

Fake Locust Biscuits

Water was hard for Abraham and his family to find in the desert. They also didn't have a large variety of fruits and vegetables to choose from. What they did have in large supply, though, were insects! There were so many grasshoppers and locusts that Abraham and his family cooked them and ate them. They fried grasshoppers in oil. They boiled locusts in salted water. They even ground up locusts and mixed them with flour and honey to make biscuits! You can make locust biscuits too, but instead of bugs, you can use almonds.

12 biscuits

 (Adult help suggested.)

Preheat oven to 450°.

Place the vegetable shortening, flour, baking powder, and salt into a large mixing bowl. Use a fork to mix the ingredients together until the mixture looks like small crumbs.

Ingredients

$^1/_3$ cup vegetable shortening

$1^3/_4$ cups flour

$2^1/_2$ teaspoons baking powder

$^3/_4$ teaspoon salt

$^1/_4$ cup sliced almonds

$^3/_4$ cup milk

Butter

Honey

Utensils

Measuring cup

Measuring spoons

Large mixing bowl

Fork

Nongrooved drinking glass (plastic)

Cookie sheet

Crumble the sliced almonds into small pieces by hand, or use a food processor to chop them. Add these to the flour crumbs, and mix in with the fork.

Stir in enough milk to form a ball with the dough. Knead this ball with your hands for a minute.

Sprinkle some flour on the countertop, place the ball of dough on the counter, and pat it into a large flat circle that is a half-inch thick. You can use a non-grooved drinking glass for this. Use the opening of the drinking glass to cut the dough into circles. Place these circles on an ungreased cookie sheet. Bake for 10 minutes.

To eat, break the biscuits in half and serve with butter and honey.

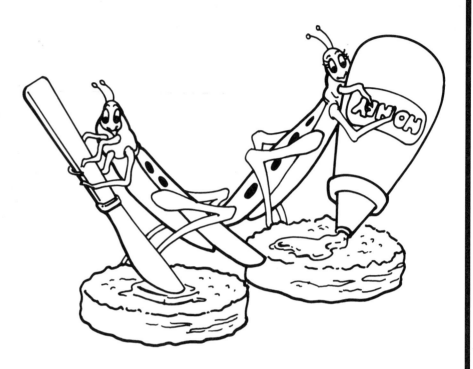

SHEEP, GOATS, LIONS, AND BEARS GAME

Isaac, like every young boy of his day, probably spent many hours keeping watch over his father's sheep and goats. As their shepherd, he stayed on the lookout for wild animals hunting for a tasty meal. Shepherd boys became good shots with a desert rock and could chase away lions or bears by throwing rocks at them if they came too close to the flocks.

Materials

Watch with a second hand

Small playing field, with boundaries marked at 10 or 20 feet

10 to 30 players

 To play this game, one person is designated as the shepherd. The shepherd is the timekeeper and holds the watch. The players divide into two groups, half as sheep or goats, the other half as lions or bears. (For a large group of players, have all the lions and bears wear a loose string of yarn tied like a necklace around their necks so they are identifiable.)

The sheep (or goats) stand on one side of the playing field and the lions (or bears) stand on the other. When the shepherd signals to begin, the lions try to tag the sheep. The players must act like the animals they're representing, and there is no running. When a sheep is tagged, the lion escorts the sheep outside the marked boundaries and then returns to try to tag another animal. The shepherd signals for the game to stop after 30 seconds for a large group of players. Small groups may play longer.

lions or
bears

shepherd

lions or bears
out of the
game

sheep or
goats

At this point, all the tagged sheep (or goats) become lions (or bears). All lions (or bears) who didn't tag an animal are out of the game. The players stand on either side of the field again, and the game is played as before.

The game is played until all players are out of the game. In between each round, observe how the numbers of each kind of animal change. Compare this to the number of animals before that particular round was played. Is there a pattern? When the game is finished, discuss how everyone ended up being the same type of animal and why. Relate your observations to animals living in the wild today. For instance, if all the food animals are killed, the hunters overpopulate and die out, too, from starvation.

Research has shown that even though Abraham didn't realize it at the time, when he and his family lived in different areas and killed the wild animals to protect their sheep and goats, the wild animals started on the road to extinction. Many wild animals living in Abraham's homeland 4,000 years ago can't be found living wild in the Middle East today.

APPEARANCE AND CLOTHING

What did Abraham and his family look like? What kind of clothes did they wear? Did boys dress differently from girls?

Isaac's physical appearance was a lot like that of the rest of the people who lived in the hot, dry desert. His dark skin was burned even darker from the sun since they didn't have sunscreen as we do today. He probably used olive oil, though, to rub all over his skin and hair. This helped his skin not to dry out. It also helped kill lice, a pesky problem for people living in the desert.

Isaac's nose was probably flat. His hair was long and black. He and his family were short. In fact, his father, Abraham, was probably only five feet tall!

How do we know what Isaac and his family looked like? Archaeologists have found pictures of people in the tombs of Egyptian pharaohs. These pictures show people who weren't Egyptians but were living in Egypt. These pictures show us what Abraham and his family probably looked like since they visited Egypt and were neighbors with the Egyptians.

Isaac, along with the other boys and girls he knew, wore clothes similar to those his parents wore. Most people didn't wear underwear, although they sometimes wore loincloths. Everyone, though, wore a *tunic*. (Say it: TWO-nick.) A tunic was loose fitting and looked like a very simple dress. Girls wore tunics that reached to their ankles. The necks of their tunics were decorated with pretty embroidery. Often, the embroidery pattern or design showed which village the girl was from. The fabric of a girl's tunic was usually blue. Boys wore tunics that usually hung down just to their knees. The fabric was made of different colors and often had stripes.

Servants probably wove the fabric that made the clothes for Abraham and his family, but if Abraham wanted to purchase a new tunic at the marketplace, he would buy one that didn't have an opening for his head. This showed that the tunic was brand-new and hadn't been worn yet. He would make a V-shaped cut in the tunic for his head to fit through.

Everyone wore a belt made from fabric. Girls wore belts that were different colors. Boys tucked weapons or small hand tools into their belts. If they wanted to carry money, they'd cut a slit in their belts and put the coins inside. If Isaac needed to run quickly after his father's sheep, he would fold up the bottom of his tunic and tuck it into his belt.

Boys and girls wore cloaks, or robes, over their tunics when it was cold if their parents were wealthy and could afford the extra outfit. They wore leather sandals or slippers if they didn't go barefoot.

Most people wore some sort of a hat to shield themselves from the hot sun. Men like Isaac's father, Abraham, probably wore a cap with extra fabric folded around it that looked like a turban. Isaac's mother, Sarah, wore a flat length of fabric folded in the front to shield her eyes from the desert sun. The fabric fell down the back of her head and over her neck. She wore a cord or beaded band around her forehead to hold the fabric head covering in place.

Make a Girl's Outfit

If a pillowcase is the right size for you to wear, use a pencil to draw a V-shape at the closed end. This is where your head will fit through. Cut this out. Cut two armholes, one on either side of the V-shaped hole in the pillow seam. Along the edges of the V-shaped opening, glue decorative lace or rickrack. Slip the pillowcase over your head to wear the tunic.

If you can't wear a pillowcase, cut a sheet into a large rectangle. When folded in half, the rectangle should extend from your shoulders to your ankles. It should be slightly wider than your shoulder width, as tunics were loose fitting. Fold the rectangle in half,

Materials

Blue pillowcase or sheet

Pencil

Scissors

Fabric glue

Lace, rickrack, or other colorful trim

Tape measure

$1/2$ yard brightly colored knit fabric

Sandals

Jewelry

To make the belt, cut a 6-inch by 3-foot piece of knit fabric. Fold the fabric in half lengthwise and glue the edges together.

For the head covering, cut a 2-foot square piece from the sheet. Drape the head covering over your head so that it shields your eyes from the sun and flows down behind your neck. Tie on a strip of knit fabric around your forehead to hold the head covering in place.

Wear sandals and jewelry to complete your outfit.

gluing the sides together. Leave a 12-inch opening at the top of each side for your arms. Cut a V-shaped opening in the center of the fold for your head to fit through. Along the edges of the V-shaped opening, glue decorative lace or rickrack.

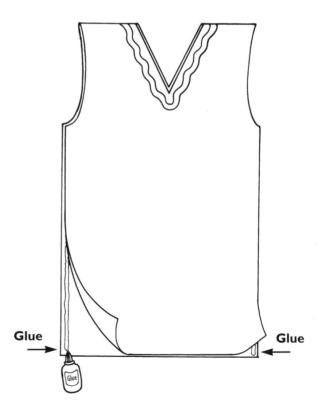

Glue →   ← Glue

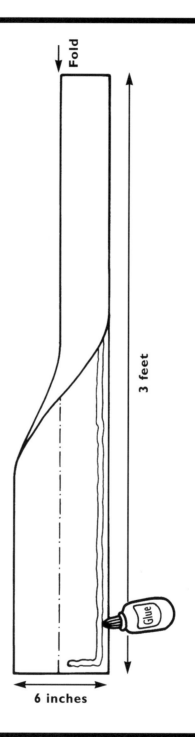

Fold

3 feet

6 inches

Glue

Make a Boy's Outfit

Follow the basic instructions to make the girl's tunic. Don't add decorative trim around the neck opening. Your tunic should only come down to your knees.

Materials

Pillowcase or sheet,
striped or solid colored

Pencil

Scissors

Tape measure

Knit fabric

Fabric glue

Bathrobe

Sandals

To make the belt, cut a six-inch by three-foot piece of knit fabric. Fold the fabric in half lengthwise and glue the edges together. If you'd like to carry coins in your belt, carefully snip a one-inch slit horizontally across the belt, about six inches up from one end of the belt. When your belt is wrapped around your waist, the coins can be put into the slit and hang down near the bottom edge of the belt.

Put on your bathrobe and sandals to complete your outfit.

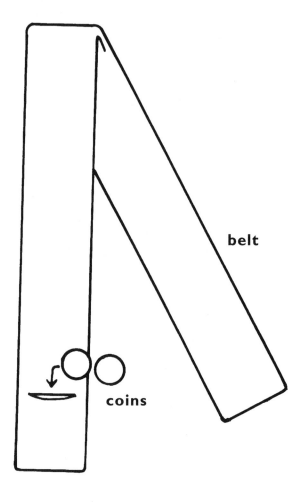

belt

coins

WEAVING WITH A LOOM

Since people made their own clothes, it took a long time to make the fabric and prepare their outfits. The wool from sheep was first twisted into thick threads that looked a lot like yarn. These threads were then tied onto a loom. Other threads were woven back and forth to create a flat piece of cloth.

One common type of loom was an upright loom. Two sturdy poles were pounded into the ground. A stick was tied across the top of the poles. Long threads were tied onto this stick. Small weights were tied onto the end of each of these threads to help keep them from getting tangled. The weaver, usually a woman or girl, sat on a stool in front of the loom. She used a flat piece of wood as a needle to weave a piece of thread back and forth across the loom.

Materials

Yarn

1 stick, about 36 inches long (a yardstick may be used)

2 chairs

Scissors

Metal washers or metal nuts

Cardboard

Tie the stick securely to the backs of the two chairs as shown in the illustration. Cut 10 four-foot pieces of yarn. Fold each yarn length in half and loop over the stick, spacing each at least 1/4-inch apart from the next. Tie a washer or nut on each end of yarn.

Cut a separate piece of yarn to weave back and forth through the yarn that is tied onto the stick. Cut a piece of cardboard to use as a needle while weaving. Cut a hole in the needle. Thread your yarn through the hole of the needle. Going from left to right, weave the needle behind a strand of yarn, in front of the next strand, and then behind the next strand of yarn. Continue weaving in and out like this until you reach the other side. Then weave back towards the left again but this time, weave your needle behind the opposite strands and in front of the opposite strands from your previous row. As you finish each row, push up the finished yarn rows tightly together to form a solid piece. Tie on new pieces of yarn to weave through your loom as the yarn in your needle is used up.

You can make a small rug on the loom. If you want to make a scarf or something longer and wider, just add more yarn or make the yarn with the weights longer. To finish off your weaving, remove the weights from the yarn and knot the 20 ends together. Cut the top of the threads off of the stick, knotting these 20 ends together. Trim any extra yarn.

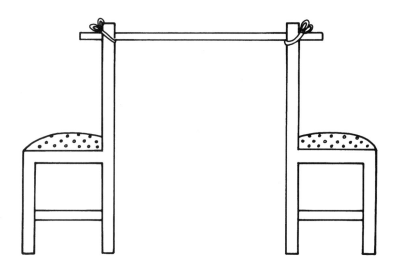

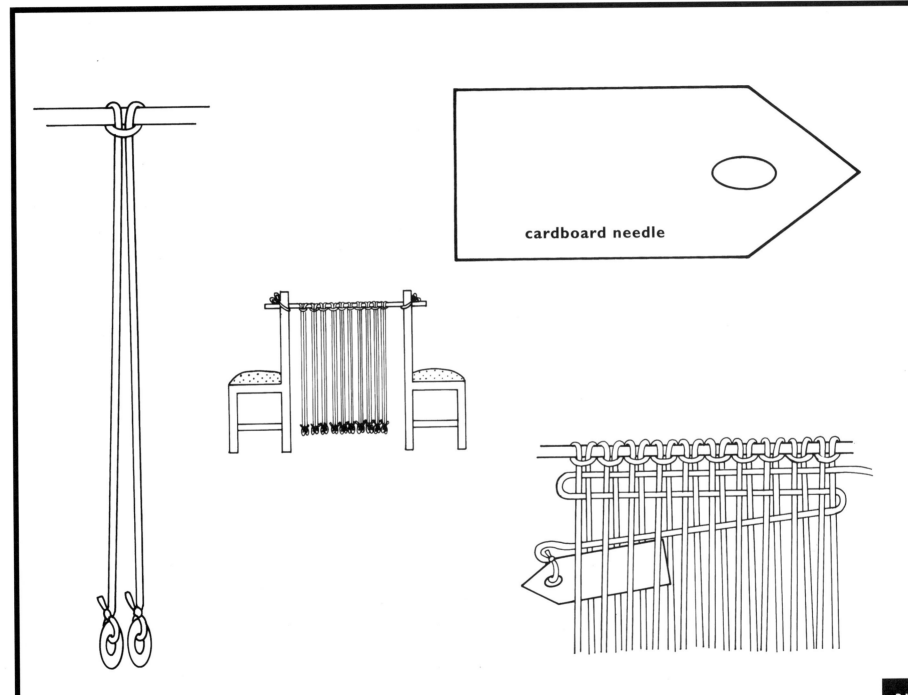

cardboard needle

31

JEWELS AND JEWELRY

uring Old Testament days, both men and women liked to wear jewelry. Women who could afford it wore jewelry to make them look beautiful. They often wore a nose ring, earrings, and arm bracelets. They had jewelry for their ankles called anklets. They wore fancy necklaces and rings. They wore pretty beads and coins across their foreheads to keep their head coverings in place. Often, their jewelry was given as marriage presents.

Men wore jewelry to show their power and importance. Chains around their necks and rings on their fingers were worn as symbols of their authority and power to make important decisions.

Materials

Pipe cleaners

Scissors

Buttons, various sizes and shapes

Hot glue gun

Jingle bells

Index card

Pennies

Glue

Hole puncher

Make a Ring

(Adult help suggested.)

To make a ring, loosely wrap a pipe cleaner around your finger. Twist the ends together and remove this twist from your finger. Cut the pipe cleaner about one inch above the twist on both ends. Slide a large two-holed flat button over the twisted part, bring the ends around, and press down flat over the button. Put the ring on your finger and adjust the pipe cleaner to form a nice loop. Remove the ring again. Ask an adult to help you use a hot glue gun to glue three more flat buttons on top of the large button to form the stone of the ring.

Decorate an Anklet

To make an anklet, thread a variety of buttons onto a 12-inch length of pipe cleaner. (Buttons with a raised loop work better than flat buttons.) Thread several jingle bells onto the pipe cleaner, between the buttons, so that the anklet resembles the ones women

buttons

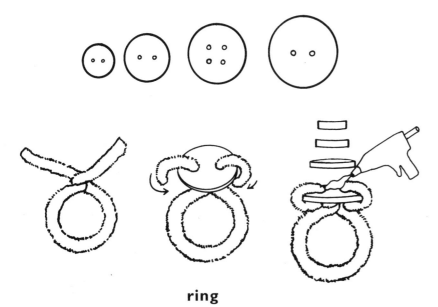

ring

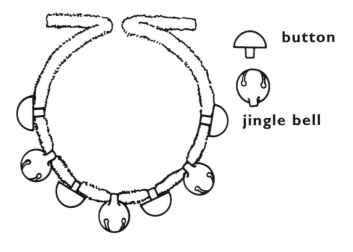

button

jingle bell

anklet

wore at this time. Their anklets made a jingling sound as they walked. After loosely filling the pipe cleaner with buttons and bells, fold back one inch on each end of the pipe cleaner so that the wire ends can be latched together to fasten the anklet to your ankle.

Design a Necklace

To make a necklace, glue rows of pennies on an index card. Punch two holes at the top of the card when the glue is dry. Cut the edges of the card off to form the pendant of the necklace. Twist two pipe cleaners together to make a long chain for your necklace. Carefully slide the pipe cleaners up through one hole on the index card and down through the other so that your penny pendant hangs on the wire. Bend and fold back one inch on each end of the pipe cleaner so the necklace can be fastened together behind your neck and worn.

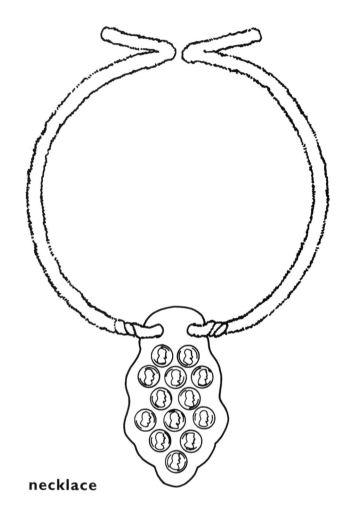

necklace

PLAY THE HOSPITALITY CARD GAME

Since Abraham and his family lived in the desert, it was a very important custom to welcome any stranger in who stopped by their tents. People could die in the desert if they weren't nourished and refreshed with food and water, or if they didn't rest occasionally out of the heat. *Hospitality*, taking care of guests and strangers, was very important to Abraham and his family, particularly because several times messengers from God had appeared at their tents looking like ordinary people. Abraham's family wanted to take care of every stranger who stopped by, especially since the visitor might be another messenger.

There were certain hospitality customs that were considered polite in Old Testament days. As you play this game, you'll learn these hospitality customs.

Materials

Illustration of hospitality cards

Paper

Pencil

Scissors

Glue

Index cards

Colored pencils

3 or more players

Photocopy or trace the hospitality cards on paper. Cut out two sets of hospitality cards. Throw away one of the host cards (you only need one for the game). Glue one hospitality card on the back of each index card. Color the pictures on the cards.

This game is similar to Old Maid. The object of the game is to try to find matching pairs for the cards in your hands. The player left holding the host card loses the game.

To play, shuffle the cards and deal them. (Players may be holding different numbers of cards.) The first player randomly chooses one card from one of the other players. If it matches one in her hand, she places the matching pair of cards on the table. The next player then takes his turn to randomly choose a card from another player. The game continues until one person is left holding the host card.

the host

Abraham, Sarah, and Isaac were the hosts, or people who invited strangers into their tent.

the bow

Visitors were greeted with a bow.

the meal

The best food was prepared and served.

their names

I wonder who he is???

It wasn't polite to ask strangers their names.

the kiss

Visiting friends were kissed on both cheeks.

their feet

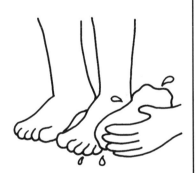

Visitors' hot, dusty feet were washed with water.

the oil

A small amount of perfumed oil was poured on the visitor's head.

the well

A stranger sat by the well waiting to be invited into others' tent homes.

the enemy

Even if the stranger was from enemy lands, it was still polite to feed him because he could die in the desert.

the messengers

Sometimes messengers were sent to visit Abraham and his family.

the tent

At night visitors were invited to sleep at the entrance of the tent for protection.

the salt

In the desert salt was as important as gold. Eating salt with a visitor showed you were peaceful.

the drink

A drink of water was given to a visitor as a sign of peace.

the animals

Animals were fed and given a safe place to sleep.

the gifts

Sometimes visitors brought gifts, such as jewelry, to give to the host.

the visit

The longer a visitor stayed, the more he showed how much he liked the host's hospitality.

RELIGIOUS BELIEFS AND ALTARS

Abraham and his family believed in one supreme being. This may not seem unusual to us today, but it was very uncommon back in the beginning of Old Testament days. Most people thought there were many different gods who were in charge of many different things. For instance, most people thought one god ruled the sun and a different god ruled the moon. Greek and Egyptian mythologies are examples of these types of beliefs. People often built statues called *idols* (say it: EYE-dolls) to represent what they thought the gods looked like, and then they prayed to the statues.

Abraham and his family were different from these people. They believed in one supreme being who they called God and who made the whole world and loved people as his own children. Abraham believed that God had called him away from the city of Ur to travel through the desert and move to the area we know today as Israel. Abraham believed that God wanted his entire family—even future generations—to live in Israel and worship God. The Jewish people living in Israel and around the world today still follow these ideas that Abraham first believed so many years ago. Israel is sometimes referred to as the "Promised Land" because God promised this land to Abraham and his family.

As Abraham left Ur and traveled through the wilderness to the land God wanted his family to live in, Abraham built altars in places that were special to him. Sometimes Abraham built an altar to remember an important conversation he held with God. He built altars for other reasons too, including to take time to be closer to God, to say he was sorry for mistakes that he or other family members had made, and to bury idols and make a recommitment to only follow God. If something important happened to Abraham, he built an altar as a way of saying "thank you" to God.

Sometimes Abraham built an altar as a place to give a sacrifice to God. A *sacrifice* was a special gift Abraham gave to God. Since Abraham raised sheep and grew grain to feed them, he often chose to sacrifice his best sheep or give the nicest grain he harvested in tribute to God. Even though a sheep or a basket of grain might not seem like a very special gift to us today, to Abraham, it was the best gift he could give.

What did the altars look like that Abraham built? They were usually just a large pile of rocks. These piles of rocks, however, lasted many, many years. In fact, when Isaac grew up and traveled through the land, or when Isaac's children or their children passed by the altars, they remembered why Abraham had built each one and stopped there to worship God, too.

Where did Abraham build his altars? Most of the time, he built an altar exactly on the spot where something important happened. For instance, after he had traveled through the desert, he finally entered the land God promised him to be his new home. Abraham built an altar there. Other times, Abraham hiked up a mountain and built an altar near the top as if standing on a mountain brought him closer to God.

MAKE A MEMORIES DISPLAY BOWL

Over the years, you'll probably take fun vacations or visit relatives in other parts of the country. To help you remember your special experiences, you can start a small rock collection. If you visit the beach, pick up a shell. If you visit your cousins, find a small, interesting rock near their house. Each time you visit a new place, collect a unique rock to remind you of that experience. Design a special bowl to display your collection. Even though you are not making an altar, your collection can help you remember things that are important to you, just as altars helped Abraham and his family remember their most important experiences with God.

Materials

1 cup liquid fabric starch

Measuring cup

Mixing bowl

Newspaper

Scissors

Newspaper, cut into $\frac{1}{2}$-inch strips

Paper bowl

Waxed paper

Red or brown paint

Paintbrush

Pour about one cup of the liquid fabric starch into a mixing bowl. Cover your tabletop with several layers of newspaper. On the protected surface, dip strips of newspaper, one at a time, into the liquid fabric starch. Squeeze off the excess and then place each strip of newspaper on the paper bowl. Cover the entire paper bowl with the newspaper strips as you would for papier-mâché. Let the bowl dry on a sheet of waxed paper. Paint the bowl with red or brown paint to resemble the clay bowls Abraham might have used.

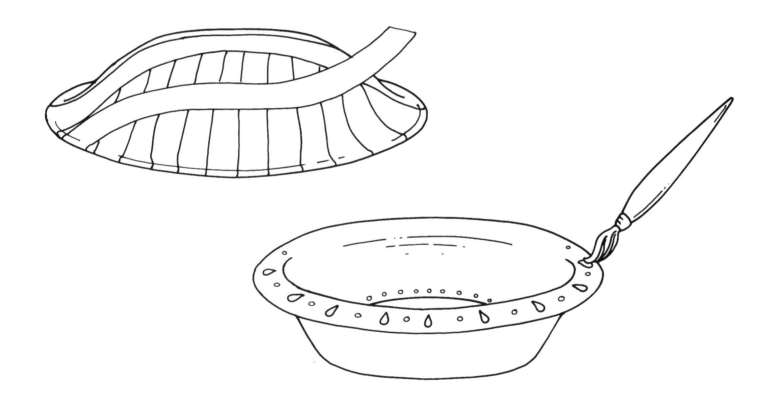

DEATH AND BURIAL TRADITIONS

Sarah and Abraham were quite old when Isaac was born. As Isaac grew up, he spent many happy years with his mother and father. Eventually, Isaac's mother died. According to the Old Testament, when Sarah died Abraham bought a field nearby that had a cave in it. Abraham used this cave as the special place to bury Sarah and other relatives who died in the following years. Abraham, himself, was buried in the same cave after he died.

When people died during Old Testament days, they had to be buried very quickly. The relatives tried to bury them within eight hours—less than half a day! This was important in the hot climate where things began to decay very fast.

The dead person's body was usually washed and then wrapped in strips of clean cloth. The body was carried on a wooden stretcher to the place where it would be buried. It was placed inside the cave on a small shelf that had been carved along the cave's wall.

A family buried many of its members in the same small cave; over the years as the bodies rotted away, the bones of each body were collected and put in special bone boxes. These boxes were kept in the back of the cave so that the shelves in the main part could be used for the bodies of the people who had just died. Outside the cave, a large rock was rolled over the opening to the cave. This rock was usually painted white to tell everyone to stay away since the cave was used only to bury people.

Since Abraham was very wealthy, he could afford to buy a field and a private cave to use as his family's burial ground. However, people who were very poor couldn't afford this and were buried in public cemeteries. These simple graveyards were kept outside the village. Often these cemeteries were made of caves.

MARRIAGE AND INHERITANCE

After Sarah died and Isaac had become an adult, Abraham decided it was time for Isaac to marry. But unlike people today, Isaac didn't fall in love and marry someone. Instead, Abraham picked one of his relatives as a suitable wife for his son.

Abraham sent his servant to visit his brother's family. The servant took camels packed with many expensive gifts Abraham wanted to give to the bride's family. In those days, traveling with camels wasn't a very common thing to do. Camels were very expensive back then! By sending his servant with a lot of camels, Abraham was telling the bride's family how wealthy he was.

When the servant arrived in the town where Abraham's relatives lived, he went to the well to get water for himself and his camels. As the servant waited, he prayed and asked God to bring Isaac's future wife to the well.

Soon thereafter Rebekah walked up to the well, and the servant discovered she was related to Abraham's brother. After visiting with her family and giving them gifts, the servant brought Rebekah back to Isaac to be married.

A short time later, Abraham died and Isaac inherited his father's great wealth. In Old Testament days, a father's wealth and land were given to his oldest son.

Isaac and Rebekah had twin sons named Esau and Jacob. Esau was born first and should have inherited their father's wealth, but when the boys grew up, Jacob tricked Esau into giving his inheritance away. This inheritance was called a *birthright*. One day Jacob was cooking a tasty meal of lentil stew (see the recipe on pages 17–18). Esau had been out in the fields hunting all day. When Esau returned home, he was so hungry he felt as if he was starving. When Esau smelled the good food cooking, he asked Jacob to share it with him. Jacob told Esau that he could have a bowl of lentil stew if Esau sold his birthright to him. Esau agreed to give Jacob his birthright in exchange for the soup. Later, Rebekah helped Jacob trick Isaac into officially giving him Esau's birthright.

After Jacob tricked Esau, however, Jacob was afraid Esau would murder him, so he ran away while Esau stayed home. Where did Jacob go? He ran back to the land where his mother's relatives lived. Now poor and without any possessions, Jacob worked many long years for his uncle, caring for his sheep and goats. While there, Jacob married two of his uncle's daughters, first Leah and then Rachel.

In Old Testament days, it wasn't unusual for men to marry more than one wife. Men wanted a lot of children. They thought that having a large family meant they had a large number of blessings. Also, children often died at a very young age in those days, so men wanted to have a lot of children in case some of them died.

Today in the United States men and women are thought of as equals. They work together in their marriage to build a happy home. But it was very different in Old Testament days. A man was the head of his family. His wife was his property. Often, she had to call him "Master." But even though these customs were different from ours, a husband usually loved his wife very much, just as a husband does today.

INTO EGYPT AND OUT AGAIN

Way Down in Egypt's Land

After living many years with his mother's people, Jacob decided to move all his family and belongings back to the land where he had been born. One evening on the journey home, Jacob helped his wives and children cross a stream. Jacob crossed back and had his servants take the rest of his possessions across the stream to make a camp for his family to spend the night. Jacob stayed by himself all night on the original side of the stream. During the night, God met Jacob and wrestled with him. They wrestled the whole night. When the sun started to rise in the morning, Jacob asked God to bless him. God gave Jacob his blessing and said that Jacob's name was now changed to Israel, which means "having wrestled with God and prevailed." (Say it: pre-VALE. *Prevail* means to succeed or have power.) From then on, all of Jacob's children and their children and their children were called Israelites.

Israel had twelve sons. Israel loved his son Joseph more than the rest. Joseph's older brothers grew jealous when this became apparent, so they sold him as a slave to a caravan of men traveling to Egypt. They, in turn, sold him to a palace official and Joseph became a slave in the palace of the *Pharaoh* (say it: FAY-ro). In time, Joseph became an important palace official himself.

For a long time, it didn't rain in and around Egypt. No crops grew. Many people starved to death. Israel's sons traveled to Egypt to buy grain for their bread. They didn't recognize their brother Joseph as the man who sold them grain, but Joseph recognized them. After Joseph told his brothers who he was, his brothers explained how sorry they were for selling him into slavery. Joseph forgave them and invited them to stay in Egypt as Pharaoh's guests. Eventually the brothers along with their father, Israel, and their wives and children settled in the land of Egypt.

After many years, Joseph died and the new Pharaoh forgot about him. The new Pharaoh didn't remember that the Israelites had been invited to live in Egypt. This Pharaoh decided to make all the Israelites slaves and force them to work on his building projects. The Israelites and their children worked very hard and under terrible conditions to make bricks out of mud and straw. Pharaoh used these bricks to build many cities.

BAKING BRICKS

Do you want to do a messy project that's great for the backyard on a summer afternoon? Pretend you're an Israelite slave and Pharaoh has ordered you to make hundreds and hundreds of bricks to bake in the hot Egyptian sun. Here's how you'd make the bricks.

Spread several handfuls of clay over the bottom of the empty wading pool. Barely cover the clay with water and let it soak for several hours. When it is soft, wade barefoot in the pool, treading on the clay to squish it up and help it dissolve. Shovel in an equal amount of dirt to the clay and continue mixing it with your feet, adding a little water if needed. Add one handful of straw at a time, treading the mixture with your feet. Add an equal

Materials

Clay soil (If there is no clay soil in your region of the country, you may use terra-cotta clay or natural clay that can be fired in a kiln.)

Small wading pool

Water

Shovels

Dirt (not potting soil)

Straw (from a feed store)

Sand

Shoe boxes or individual-sized milk cartons

amount of sand, a little bit at a time, mixing until the mud is the consistency of cookie dough.

Scoop this mixture up and pack it into shoe boxes or milk cartons to make bricks. Set the bricks in the sun to dry. When dry, tear away the cardboard from the bricks and try stacking them together. Use a mixture of clay, sand, and water (the consistency of thick mud) to hold the bricks together.

When Pharaoh was angry or wanted to punish the Israelite slaves, he ordered them to make bricks without using any straw. Try to make some bricks without any straw and discover why this was very hard for the Israelites to do.

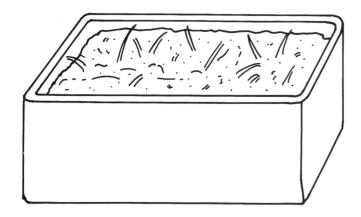

Fill a milk carton with the mixture.

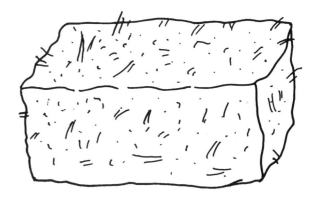

dried brick

THE NEW PRINCE OF EGYPT

Because Pharaoh didn't want there to be enough Israelite slaves to make an army to fight against him, Pharaoh ordered his soldiers to kill all the Israelite baby boys. But one day, a baby boy was born to a young Israelite woman named Jocheved. To save her son, she placed him in a basket and floated him on the Nile River in a place where she knew Pharoah's daughter bathed. (Most people bathed in the river since there weren't bathtubs or showers like those we use.)

When Pharaoh's daughter walked down to the Nile to take her bath, she discovered the basket floating on the river and asked one of her maids to open it. They found the baby inside. The princess loved the baby and named him Moses. Moses' older sister Miriam, who had watched the princess pick him up from the basket, asked the princess if Moses' real mother could help care for the baby (without revealing her identity). The princess agreed. The princess adopted Moses as her own son. As Moses grew up in the courts of Pharaoh, he was treated like a little prince.

Unlike the slaves and their children who had to constantly work, boys and girls growing up in Pharaoh's palace spent time playing with their toys. Girls played with wooden paddle dolls with hair made from clay beads. Boys practiced hitting targets with their serpent-headed throwing sticks.

EGYPTIAN PADDLE DOLL

Can you imagine trying to cuddle with a wooden doll if you were a child growing up in Pharaoh's courts?

Paint the top third of the cardboard tan for the doll's face. Paint the rest of the cardboard white for the dress. (Egyptians mostly wore white clothes because the color white kept them cooler in the hot sun.) When the paint is dry, use a thin paintbrush to paint a brown almond-shaped eye on the doll. Add a brown nose and a red mouth. Paint a colorful zigzag collar on the doll's dress and decorate the collar with spots. This doll is designed to look like the paintings of the Egyptians that have been found in the tombs of Egypt.

Materials

I 4 by 12-inch piece corrugated cardboard

Acrylic craft paints (tan, white, black, red, and other colors)

Paintbrushes

Heavy thread

Scissors

Ruler

Small beads

Pencil

For the hair of the doll, thread three 12-inch lengths of thread with small beads, loop the thread over the last bead tying a knot between the last two beads to secure each end. Lay the three lengths of beaded string on top of each other. Tie an 8-inch length of thread securely around the center of all three beaded strings and tie in a knot. With a pencil, poke a small hole in the doll's head as shown. Tie the beaded hair to the hole on the paddle doll.

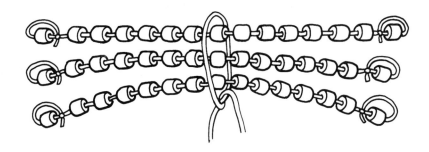

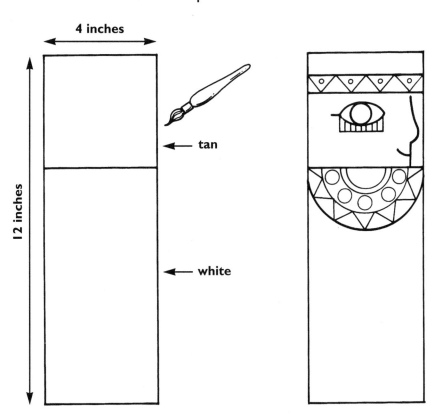

4 inches

12 inches

tan

white

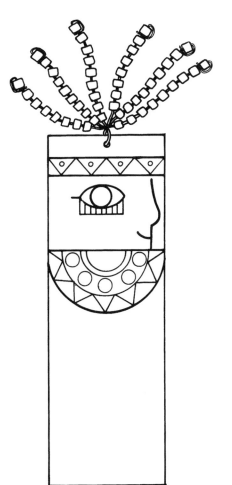

SERPENT-HEADED THROWING STICK

Boys from wealthy Egyptian families learned how to throw a special stick that was designed with the head of a snake. Moses probably spent many hours practicing with his stick trying to hit a target. Skillful hunters used these sticks to hunt birds.

Paint the spoon head a solid color. Paint the handle with stripes. Stand the spoon up in a piece of Styrofoam or in an egg carton to dry.

Paint the head of a snake on the back side of the spoon. Add designs on the handle. If you want the snake to have a tongue, glue on a short piece of red ribbon that has a slit at the end. Set up targets and practice hitting them with the stick. Invite a friend to join you in a target practice game. Each time you hit a target, you score 5 points. The first to get 20 points wins the game.

Materials

Wooden spoon

Acrylic craft paints

Paintbrushes

Piece of Styrofoam or egg carton

Red ribbon

Glue

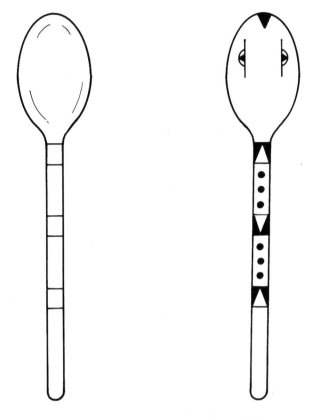

serpent-headed throwing stick

When Moses grew older, he learned that he was an Israelite and not an Egyptian. One day Moses was watching the Israelite slaves work. He saw an Egyptian beating a slave, one of Moses' own people. Moses killed the Egyptian to protect the slave. Suddenly, though, Moses felt afraid. Would Pharaoh kill him as punishment? Fearful for his life, Moses ran away from Egypt. He lived in a nearby place named Midian where he became a shepherd and carried a tall wooden stick called a shepherd's staff. One day Moses was in the desert herding his sheep when God spoke to him in a special way. God spoke to Moses from a burning bush that had flames coming from it, but the bush never burned up. God told Moses to go back to Egypt and lead the Israelites out of Egypt so they wouldn't be slaves any longer. God also told Moses that he would meet his true brother, Aaron, on his way back to Egypt. God told him that Aaron would help Moses talk to Pharaoh about setting the Israelite slaves free.

On his way back to Egypt, Moses did meet Aaron, just as God had said he would. Moses and Aaron spoke with Pharaoh. Aaron threw down his staff on the ground, and it changed into a real snake! Even after this miracle, though, Pharaoh refused to let the slaves go free. Pharaoh wanted to keep the Israelites as slaves to build more cities for him.

FREE AT LAST

God sent all sorts of troubles to the Egyptians, but still Pharaoh refused to let the Israelites go free. Finally, God told Moses that the time had arrived for the Israelites to escape. God instructed Moses to tell all the Israelites to quickly pack everything up and prepare to leave. Moses instructed the people to eat their bread with their sandals on and their walking sticks in their hands. He even told them to eat with their cloaks tucked into their belts. (Men tucked their cloaks up into their belts when they ran so the fabric wouldn't get tangled up in their legs.) Moses also instructed the Israelites to place the blood of a lamb on their doorposts. When they heard these instructions, the Israelites knew that the time had come to escape quickly from Egypt.

That night, all the Egyptians' first-born sons died from a plague sent by God, but the Israelites were saved because of the lambs' blood. Even Pharaoh's eldest son died. In the middle of the night, Pharaoh called Moses and Aaron to his throne. The Egyptians were afraid they were all going to die because of the Israelites' God, so Pharaoh told Moses to take all the Israelites and leave the land of Egypt! Their journey out of Egypt had begun.

UNLEAVENED BREAD

Ever since the night the Israelites left Egypt, a holiday has been celebrated to remember this special event. This holiday is called Passover, because the angel of death passed over the Israelites' homes. It is still celebrated today.

Moses instructed the people to quickly pack and be ready to leave at a moment's notice. He told them to make bread without yeast. Bread made with yeast took a long time to bake, but without yeast, bread could be made very quickly. Bread made without yeast is called *unleavened*.

12 servings

Ingredients

2 cups flour

1 teaspoon salt

1/2 cup milk

1/4 cup oil

2 tablespoons honey

Utensils

2 mixing bowls

Measuring cups

Measuring spoons

2 mixing spoons

Fork

Cookie sheet

(Adult help suggested.)

Preheat oven to 375°. Mix the flour and the salt in a bowl. In a separate bowl, stir together the milk, oil, and honey. Add this to the flour and salt mixture and mix well with your hands.

On a lightly floured countertop, knead the dough a bit longer and then separate it into 5-inch circles and pat down. Use a fork to flatten the circles and prick a few holes in each circle. Place these circles onto an ungreased cookie sheet. Bake the unleavened bread for 20 minutes. When cool, enjoy it with jelly, honey, or butter on top.

unleavened bread

NO YEAST GAME

To celebrate the Passover every year, the Israelites were instructed to remove all the yeast from their houses and not eat anything with yeast in it for seven days to commemorate their journey out of Egypt (slavery) to Israel (freedom). Family members carefully searched their home for yeast and threw it away. If people ate yeast during these seven days, they would be expelled from the rest of the Israelites. Today, observant Jews still rid their houses of products made with yeast in preparation for Passover.

To play this game, one player hides the packet of yeast somewhere in the kitchen. The other players then try to find the package of yeast. The person who finds the yeast gets to be the next one to hide it.

Materials

1 package yeast

2 or more players

CAMPING IN THE DESERT

After the Israelites escaped from being Pharaoh's slaves, Moses led them back into the desert where Abraham and Isaac had lived so many years before. There was just one problem, though. The Israelites had been slaves for so many years that they didn't know how to do many things. They didn't know how to organize, appoint leaders, or fight a war.

God spent a long time giving Moses instructions to help the Israelites. One of the first things they were instructed to do was to arrange their tents in a certain order. This arrangement helped keep the many Israelites organized so they wouldn't argue about where to place their tents. The Israelite people were divided into tribes named after Israel's sons. Every night when they stopped to rest, their tents were arranged according to the different tribes. In the middle of the group stood a tent called the Tabernacle (say it: TAB-er-NACK-el). The Tabernacle was used as a special meeting place to worship God. The tribe of Levi set their tents up closest to the Tabernacle because this tribe was made up of priests who took care of the Tabernacle. Moses and Aaron also had their tents set up right next to it.

THE MAP OF THE ISRAELITE CAMP

Each tribe had a unique campsite in relation to the Tabernacle. Whenever the group moved to a new campsite, each tribe knew where to pitch its tent around the Tabernacle so that setting up camp was orderly and the Tabernacle was protected by tribal groups on all sides.

Joseph's name is missing because he had two sons and therefore two half-tribes, one named after each. These are the tribes of Ephraim and Manasseh.

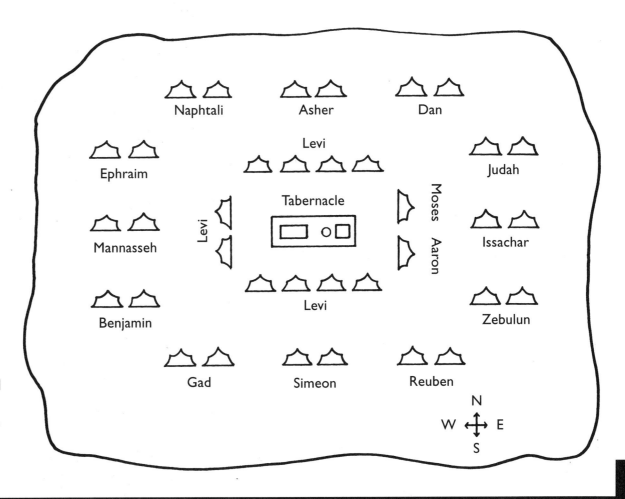

THE TEN COMMANDMENTS

he Israelites pitched their tents near a mountain known as Mount Sinai (say it: SIGN-eye). At Mount Sinai, Moses received the Ten Commandments. Carved on stone tablets, the Ten Commandments were 10 laws written down for the people to follow.

Materials

Oven-bake clay (found in craft stores)

Rolling pin

Plastic knife

Toothpick

Cookie sheet

 (Adult help suggested.)

Preheat the oven to 275°. Flatten a lump of clay that is the size of a golf ball. Roll it out until it's about four inches square. Use the knife and follow the illustration to cut the shape of stone tablets from the clay.

Use the toothpick to carve the Hebrew numbers 1 through 10 onto the clay tablets. Carefully place the clay tablets onto the cookie sheet.

Bake for 15 minutes. Let cool before removing from the cookie sheet.

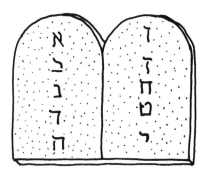

clay tablets

MOSES THE LAWGIVER

Moses wrote down more than six hundred laws that God gave him to help govern the Israelites. These laws instructed the Israelites to do many things, such as to take a lost donkey back to its owner, even if the owner was one of their enemies. Another law said they should celebrate the Feast of Unleavened Bread by eating bread made without yeast for seven days. Another law said they couldn't light a fire in their home on the seventh day of the week because God rested on the seventh day of creation. Today, these laws can be found in the first books of the Old Testament.

When you first look at them, these laws seem like a huge number of complicated things to do!

But to the Israelite people, who had been slaves for many years, these laws were very practical and helpful as they tried to live their own lives in freedom. Many of the laws explained how to keep their camp clean and their people healthy from disease. Since there weren't many doctors at that time and only a few dentists, these laws were very important to help the people stay alive.

Since the Israelites didn't have any police officers, other laws explained how to take care of thieves, criminals, and different kinds of crimes. These laws also gave rules concerning marriages and inheritance so that the people could be treated fairly.

A DOCTOR'S KIT

The few doctors there were had to help people with all kinds of diseases. Children in Old Testament days suffered from many illnesses that American children hardly ever get because of modern vaccines. Israelite children died from dysentery and cholera (infections that caused terrible diarrhea), typhoid (an infection from drinking bad water that caused high fevers), beriberi (lack of vitamins causing people to become paralyzed), and leprosy (a bad skin disease). In the dry desert, children often had worms from the water they drank or eye infections from the flies.

A doctor's kit in Old Testament days looked very different from a doctor's kit used today—almost all the items in the Old Testament kit came from the kitchen. That's because most medicine was made from common things the people already had. The Israelites also used wine and herbs for treating such things as stomachaches and headaches.

If you lived during Old Testament days, you would use olive oil to wash a sick person's head. You would spread honey over a cut with a tool that looked a lot like three paintbrushes held together with rubber bands. You would rub yeast on a baby's hurting gums or give garlic to someone with a toothache. (Caution: Don't try these remedies on yourself or friends.)

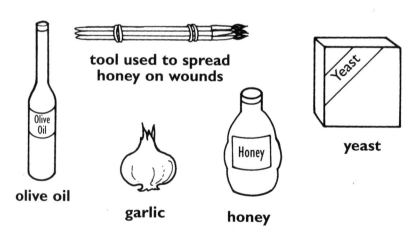

tool used to spread
honey on wounds

olive oil

garlic

honey

yeast

LEPROSY

Leprosy was a skin disease that many people got during Old Testament days. People with leprosy always died. People in poor countries still suffer from leprosy today, although there are many medicines now to help stop this horrible disease. Leprosy was so bad during Old Testament days that many, many laws were written to help people from catching it from each other. Some of the laws were written so that everyone knew exactly which people had leprosy. Lepers had to cover the lower part of their faces with a cloth. They couldn't brush their hair or wear a hat or head covering as most people did. They had to tear their clothes. They even had to live far away from healthy people. Lepers often lived in their own groups where they could help each other. If they saw anyone who wasn't a leper, they had to shout, "Unclean!" so that the healthy person knew to stay far away from them.

THE SABBATH LAWS

Some of the laws that Moses wrote down told the Israelites how to build the Tabernacle. The Tabernacle was the tent where people worshiped God. These laws about the Tabernacle also explained how the people were supposed to worship God so that they could follow God's ways and not do wrong things that hurt other people.

The most important day of the week for the Israelites was the *Sabbath* (say it: SAB-ith). Many laws were written about the observance of the Sabbath so that the Israelites could spend this day worshiping God instead of doing other things.

The Sabbath started at sundown on Friday night. It lasted until Saturday evening when three stars could be seen in the darkened sky.

To tell the people when the Sabbath started and finished, a loud horn was blown.

Everyone was expected to follow the laws of the Sabbath, even the children. On the Sabbath, nobody was allowed to do any work because God rested on the seventh day of creation. They were supposed to spend this holy day worshiping God.

To get ready for the Sabbath, the children had to work extra hard during the day on Friday. They had to help their parents clean up the tents so they wouldn't have to clean on the Sabbath. They helped their parents cook extra food so they wouldn't have to cook on the Sabbath. Most of the time, they washed and dressed up in their very best clothes as Friday night drew closer. They wanted to look their very best so they could honor God.

MAKING A TRUMPET

During Old Testament days, trumpets were often made from the horns of sheep. This type of trumpet was called a *shofar* (say it: show-far). The shofar was used to give signals. It wasn't used to make music. The Israelites used the shofar to signal many things, such as the starting of the Sabbath, calling people to battle, or scaring away their enemies.

Ask someone to help you wrap the sheet of poster board into a cone. One end should be smaller, about 1/2-inch wide. The other end should be larger, about 3 inches wide. Tape the shofar together. Trim the larger end so the edge of the shofar is even.

Snip the very tip of the rounded end off of the balloon (not the end where you blow it up). Pull the balloon into the smaller end of the cone, cut end in

first. Fold the other edge of the balloon (the edge you blow in) out of the smaller cone end and fold it so that it covers about 1/2 inch on the outside of the poster board. Tape this edge in place.

Materials

1 8½ by 11-inch piece
poster board

Ruler

Scissors

1 7-inch balloon

Wide clear tape

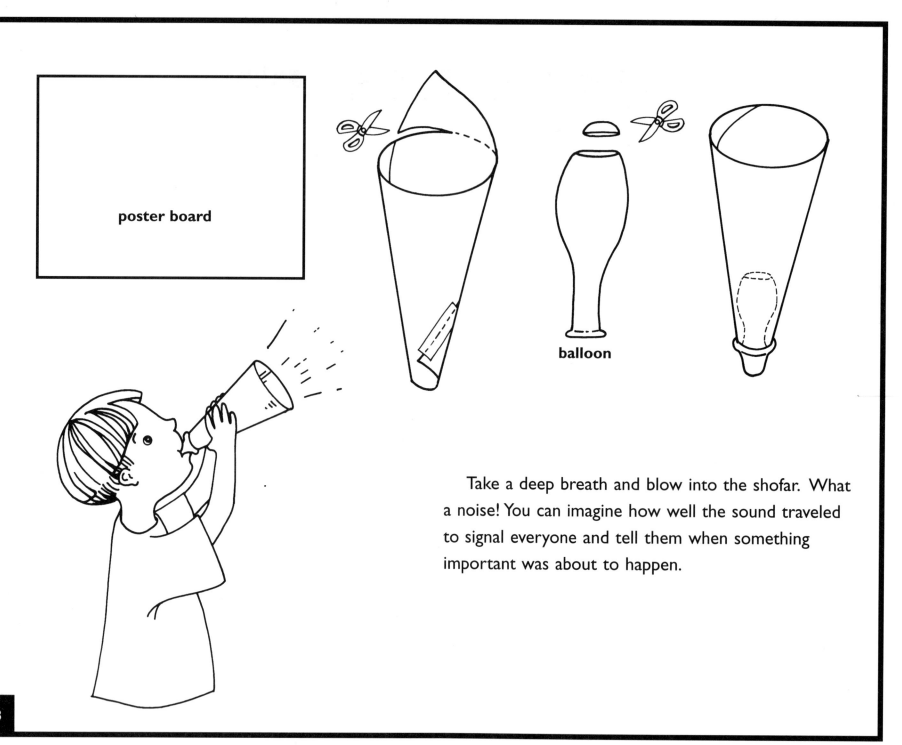

poster board

balloon

Take a deep breath and blow into the shofar. What a noise! You can imagine how well the sound traveled to signal everyone and tell them when something important was about to happen.

THE TABERNACLE

The Tabernacle was first built after Moses received the Ten Commandments. Since the Israelites were traveling from Egypt to the new land that God had promised them, they needed to carry the Tabernacle with them. Everything in the Tabernacle could be carried, including the furniture such as the Ark and the Altar of Incense. These pieces of furniture had long poles on both sides so they could be picked up and carried.

When the Israelites reached a new campsite, they set up the Tabernacle in the center of all their tents to protect it and to show that the Tabernacle and worshiping God were the most important things in their lives.

The Tabernacle was a tent hung over a frame of gold-covered wood. The wooden frame was covered with beautifully decorated curtains with embroidered pictures of cherubim (say it: CHAIR-a-bim).

Cherubim were special kinds of angels. The Old Testament doesn't really explain what these angels looked like, but some scholars think they looked like lions with wings.

Curtains made of goatskin covered the top of the Tabernacle. These curtains were covered with another curtain made from sheep and badger skins. This top curtain was painted red.

The Tabernacle stood inside a large yard surrounded by a fence made from posts hung with more curtains. Inside this large courtyard also stood the Altar of Burnt Offerings. A bronze basin stood in front of the Tabernacle. It was the priests' job to wash themselves at the bronze basin and then prepare the animal sacrifices to burn on the Altar of Burnt Offerings. The Israelites sacrificed goats, lambs, bulls, and other animals as offerings to God according to the laws that Moses gave them.

There were two rooms inside the Tabernacle. In the first room stood the Altar of Incense, the table, and the lamp stand. Incense was burned every morning and evening on the Altar of Incense. Every Sabbath, 12 loaves of bread were put on the table for the 12 tribes of Israel. These loaves were kept on the table at all times to show everyone that God was always generous. Every Sabbath, the priests ate the 12 loaves of bread and 12 new loaves were put in their place.

In the second room, called the Holy of Holies, the Ark of the Covenant was kept. Only the High Priest could go into the Holy of Holies, and he could only go in there once a year. The Ark held the stone Ten Commandments, a jar of manna, and Aaron's staff. Each of these items was very special to the Israelites. Some of their laws were written on the Ten Commandments. The manna was a special type of breadlike food God gave them in the desert when, without

it, they would have died from starvation. Aaron's staff had turned into a snake when Moses and Aaron were pleading with Pharaoh to free the slaves. The Israelites kept these three sacred objects in the Ark to help them remember the miracles that God had performed for them.

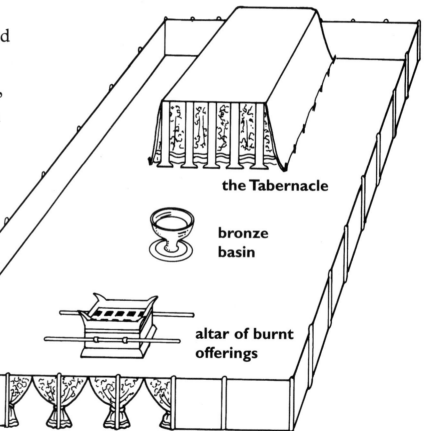

the Tabernacle

bronze basin

altar of burnt offerings

PRIESTS

It took a lot of work to take care of the Tabernacle. Aaron and his family were chosen for this important position. They were called priests.

The priests had many important jobs to do. They performed the sacrifices. They lit the lamp. They burned the incense, which made a smoky cloud of pleasant-smelling spices. They prayed for the people and taught them God's laws. The priests blew the shofar to announce important happenings. They carried the Ark when it was time to move to a new camp.

The priests wore special clothes. They wore turbans, or hats, of white linen and white linen garments underneath their tunics.

The High Priest's Outfit

The High Priest, or Most Holy Priest, wore clothes that showed he was different from the other priests. He wore a white turban with a golden plate that said "Holiness to the Lord." He wore a special breastplate that hung from his neck like a necklace. This special breastplate had the names of the 12 tribes of Israel on it. The job of High Priest was passed down through the generations from a father to his son.

The Turban

Materials

1 12 by 18-inch piece white construction paper

Scissors

Clear tape

Stapler

1 white 4-gallon plastic trash bag

Gold gift wrap or yellow construction paper

Glue

To make the High Priest's turban, cut the white construction paper lengthwise in half. Tape these two strips together at the ends. Fold them in half lengthwise and form a headband that fits around your head. Staple the ends of the headband together, cutting off the extra paper. Be sure to keep the sharp ends of the staples to the outside of the headband as you work.

Fold the bottom edge of the plastic bag's opening up about three inches and staple the opening around the inside of the headband. The bag will have a lot of gathers. Staple the two corners of the bag to the headband to give the effect of a turban. Cut a strip of gold or yellow paper and glue this around the paper headband to cover the staples.

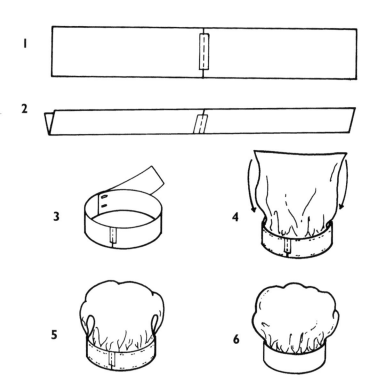

The Breastplate

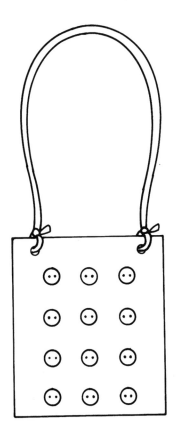

Glue the gold or yellow paper onto one side of the poster board. Use the hole puncher to punch two holes in the top corners of the breastplate. Tie a two-foot piece of ribbon through these holes so that the breastplate can be worn as a necklace. Glue the 12 buttons to the front of the breastplate.

Materials

Glue

Gold gift wrap or yellow construction paper

1 7 by 8-inch rectangle poster board

Hole puncher

Gold or yellow ribbon, $\frac{1}{2}$ inch wide

Ruler

12 flat colorful buttons, $\frac{1}{2}$ to 1 inch in diameter

breastplate

FEASTS AND FESTIVALS

The priests also helped the Israelites remember important events in their history. These events were celebrated every year as holidays with feasts and festivals. As they celebrated, the people remembered God's help in the past and God's goodness in providing their food and freedom. Children as well as their parents took part in the holidays.

There were at least six major holidays. The New Year was celebrated on the first day of the seventh month in the Israelites' calendar. The Israelites celebrated this day as a time of rest. To us, resting might seem like a dull celebration, but to children living in Old Testament days when each day was filled with hard work, a day of rest was a time of great celebration!

Two other holidays were celebrated in the seventh month—Sukkoth (or the Feast of Booths) and the Day of Atonement. For Sukkoth, everyone celebrated the end of the grape and olive harvest. Children helped build huts from branches. These huts, or booths, were built because the farms were far from their homes. During harvest, it was easier to live in these temporary shelters than to travel back and forth each day to their houses. All the people slept in these huts during the seven days of the celebration. In later years, these huts helped the Israelites remember how God cared for them in the desert on their way out of Egypt.

The Day of Atonement was the one day of the year when the High Priest walked into the Holy of Holies, the special room in the Tabernacle. He offered a sacrifice to ask God to forgive the people of their sins. All the children and their families ate no food on this special day and spent time praying to God.

Passover was celebrated to remember the time that the Israelites lived as slaves in Egypt. The Israelites celebrated Passover by cooking a special meal of lamb and unleavened bread. Eating the unleavened bread (baked without yeast) reminded the children how God brought their families safely out of Egypt and away from slavery.

First Fruits was a joyful party when the Israelites gave the season's first bunch of barley as an offering to God. Barley is a grain similar to wheat, and was a very important food to the Israelites.

The Feast of Weeks was the other important harvest festival. This holiday was celebrated exactly 50 days after Passover. It marked the end of the grain harvest and was a wonderful time of thanksgiving.

THE CALENDAR

The calendar we use today and the calendar children used during Old Testament days both have 12 months, but the common calendar used today is based on the sun while the Old Testament calendar was based on the moon. The common calendar says that a year is 365 days, the amount of time it takes the earth to travel one complete turn around the sun. The 365 days are divided into 12 months that have about the same number of days in each month. Every fourth year, an extra day is added to the calendar. When this occurs, it is called a leap year and helps keep the calendar accurate.

The calendar that was used during Old Testament days and is still used by Jews today began each month when a new moon appeared. A new moon was the first slice of moon the Israelites saw in the night sky that showed up after the moon had been dark and "invisible." Each month then lasted about 30 days, which is the amount of time it takes for a moon to progress from a new moon to a full moon and back to dark again. Since the Old Testament calendar was based on the cycle of the moon, it had 12 months with 29 or 30 days in each month. However, these months only added up to 354 days, which made the Jewish calendar 11 days shorter than the common calendar! To make their calendar even out so that the holidays stayed at the right time of year, about every three years a leap month was added during winter.

It is interesting to note that a solar eclipse always happened on the first day of the month in Old Testament days. A solar eclipse is when the moon blocks out the light from the sun because it positions itself between the earth and the sun. The moon is actually dark to us even though we can see the sun's rays from the eclipse. The moon is a new moon, which is always the first day of the month on a Jewish calendar.

Photocopy or trace the calendar on page 78 onto a piece of paper. Cut out the calendar and glue it to a paper plate. Punch a hole in the top and make a hanger with pipe cleaner or yarn. Hang the calendar next to the one your family uses to see how a year passed by for someone your age who lived during Old Testament days.

Materials

Illustration of calendar

Pencil

Tracing paper

Scissors

Glue

1 9-inch paper plate

Hole puncher

Pipe cleaners or yarn

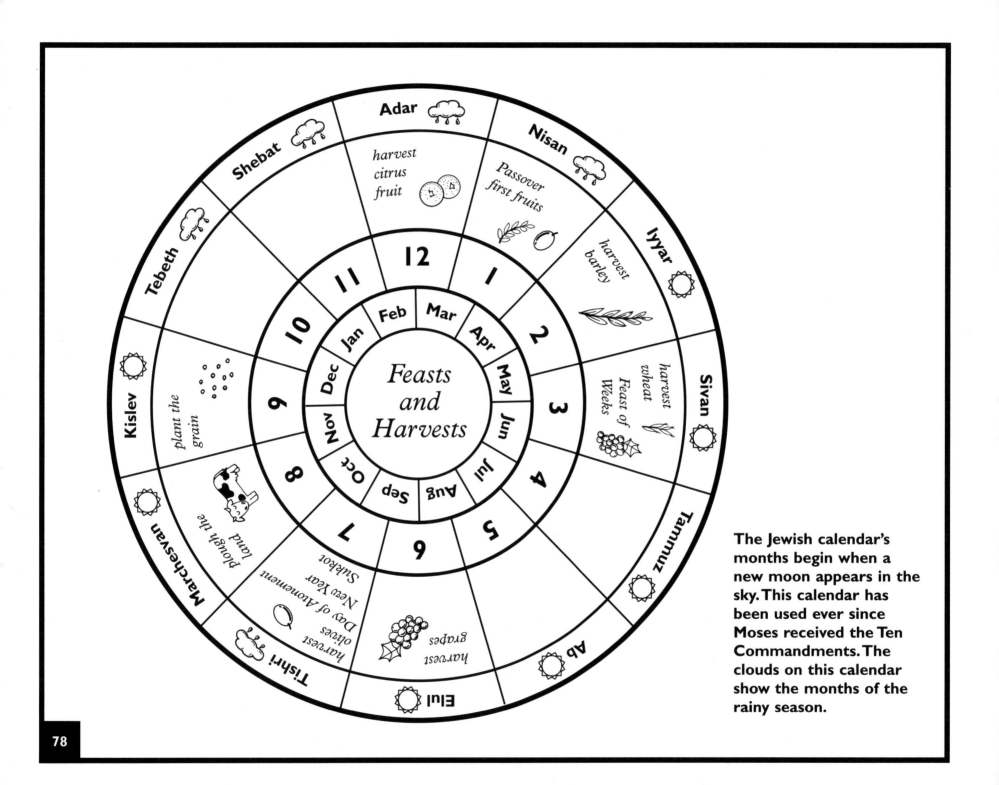

The Jewish calendar's months begin when a new moon appears in the sky. This calendar has been used ever since Moses received the Ten Commandments. The clouds on this calendar show the months of the rainy season.

THE DESERT

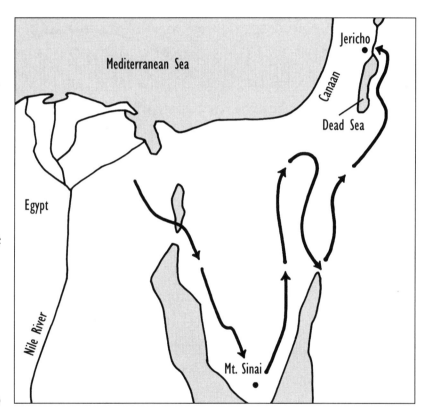

oses and the Israelites traveled through the desert camping from place to place for 40 years. They were heading for the land of Canaan. This was the special land God had promised to Abraham and his relatives. The Israelites said they were on their way to the Promised Land.

When we look at the map of the route the Israelites probably followed, it looks like they took the long way. We might wonder why they didn't walk along the shortest route to get to Canaan. They took the longer route because it was chosen by God. The easier route along the coast was heavily guarded. The Israelites would have had a hard time fighting to break through. Also, the Israelites had to learn how to follow their new laws, trust in God, and become soldiers instead of slaves. God wanted the Israelites to wander in the desert while they learned these lessons.

Probable route Moses and the Israelites traveled.

JERICHO

As the Israelites neared the Promised Land, Moses prayed and asked God to give the Israelites a new leader. God chose a man named Joshua who was known for his strong faith. Moses trained Joshua to take over the position of leading the Israelites. On the edge of the Promised Land Moses died at the ripe old age of 120! Joshua then became the leader of the Israelites. He led them across the Jordan River and into the Promised Land.

The first city the Israelites reached was Jericho. This was a key city the Israelites needed to conquer in order to enter the rest of Canaan. As far as we can tell, the city of Jericho was completely sur-rounded by a strong wall. This wall was wide enough to have entire houses built inside of it. The people living in these houses could look out of the city through windows built along the wall. There was only one gate that led into the city and out, making Jericho easier to protect.

By the time Joshua and the Israelites arrived at Jericho, this city already had a lot of history. Archaeologists have found many clues about Jericho's past. In fact, Jericho is the oldest city they've ever discovered! They think it was first built around 5000 B.C.—about 4,800 years before the Israelites first saw it.

A city in the middle of the desert, Jericho was built because there was water nearby. People settled in Jericho because of the constant supply of water. Palm trees, dates, fruits, and grain grew there since the dirt was excellent for farming. By the time Joshua and the Israelites arrived, the city of Jericho had been conquered and rebuilt many, many times.

If you were to travel to Jericho today, you'd see that this city is still very much a part of the dry desert. The original city lies in ruins now and looks like a pile of dirt and stones. Many teams of archaeologists continue to dig in these ruins and find treasures that tell us about the city's past. A modern city of Jericho is built near the ruins.

CANAAN, THE PROMISED LAND

After conquering the city of Jericho, Joshua led the Israelites into the land of Canaan. The land they found was made up of five different regions.

The first of these regions, the Transjordan, is the place Joshua and the Israelites traveled through before they came to Jericho. As its name says, it's the place "beyond the Jordan River" and is a high, flat land.

The Jordan Valley is a long, low valley stretching along the Jordan River from the Sea of Galilee to the Dead Sea. The Dead Sea is the lowest place on earth—it is 1,292 feet below sea level. The Dead Sea is very salty because there are no rivers or streams that flow out of it. The water from the Jordan River enters the Dead Sea and stays there until the hot sun makes it evaporate. As the water evaporates, it leaves a large amount of salt behind, which makes the Dead Sea very salty.

The Central Mountain Range is made up of hills and valleys. These mountains are about 3,000 feet tall.

The Coastal Plain is a narrow strip of land along the coast of the Mediterranean Sea.

South of the Dead Sea is the Desert, the fifth region of Canaan. The hot, dry sands of this desert make it almost impossible for anyone to live there.

BUILD A SALT-DOUGH MAP

As the Israelites traveled into the Promised Land, they wandered through deserts, crossed rivers, and hiked up mountains. The map illustration shows the hills and valleys they walked across in their new homeland.

Trace the map of the five regions that the Israelites found in the Promised Land. Cut out the map and glue it onto the sturdy cardboard.

In the bowl, combine the flour, salt, and water to make dough. Mix the dough well with your hands. Spread it out evenly over the map. With your fingers, form the dough into a long ridge of mountains along the Central Mountain Range. Form another long ridge of mountains along the Transjordan. Flatten the Jordan Valley between these two ranges of mountains, pressing out a line that marks the Jordan River and hollows that mark the Dead Sea and the Sea of Galilee. Flatten the Coastal Plain along the left edge of the map and the Desert along the bottom.

Materials

Illustration of map

Pencil

1 sheet typing or tracing paper

Scissors

Glue

1 8½ by 11-inch piece sturdy cardboard

Mixing bowl

1 cup flour

½ cup salt

½ cup water

5 colors paint

Paintbrush

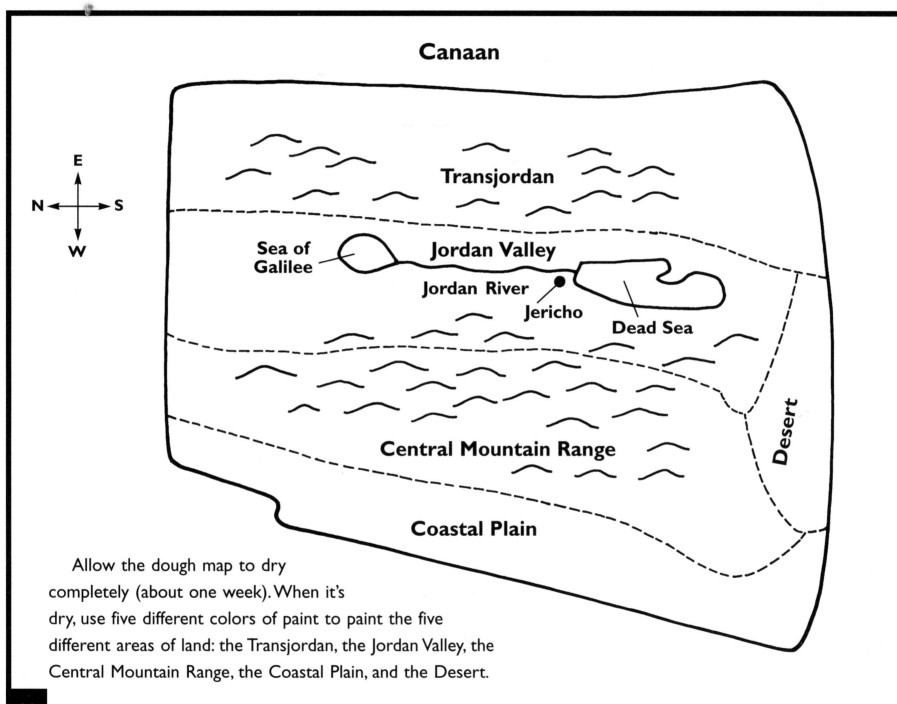

Canaan

E

N ← → S

W

Transjordan

Jordan Valley

Sea of
Galilee

Jordan River

Jericho

Dead Sea

Central Mountain Range

Desert

Coastal Plain

Allow the dough map to dry
completely (about one week). When it's
dry, use five different colors of paint to paint the five
different areas of land: the Transjordan, the Jordan Valley, the
Central Mountain Range, the Coastal Plain, and the Desert.

CONQUERING CANAAN

Joshua led the Israelite soldiers into many battles to conquer the land of Canaan. However, they didn't have many weapons to use. Most of their battles were fought with hand tools, arrows, and slings. Axes, clubs, and swords were used to fight enemies up close. The soldiers used small swords curved like a crescent moon.

The Israelites often used surprise attacks as a way to catch their enemies off guard. Sometimes they drew the people out from the city to fight, and then they burned the city down. Other times the soldiers surrounded the city and camped outside its walls. The soldiers waited for the people inside the city to run out of food and water, or to surrender. Soldiers conquered some cities by first destroying the city walls before rushing in to capture the city. Stone carvings from this time period show us some of the different tactics of war. Every healthy man was expected to join the army and fight.

ARMORED VEST

Axes were common tools among the people—used to chop wood, make farm tools, and cut animal hides—and therefore were often used as weapons in hand-to-hand combat. To protect themselves from axes and sharp arrows in battle, soldiers created armored vests from pieces of clay, metal scales, or plates that they would sew on their tunics.

(Adult help suggested.)

If a pillowcase fits you, cut out two arm-holes and one neck hole from the pillowcase as shown. If the pillowcase is too small, use the sheet to make a vest that fits you. Cut the sheet into a rectangle, fold it in half, and sew the sides. This should look like a large pillowcase. Use the pattern provided to cut out 18 armored plates from the milk jugs. Punch two holes in the top of each plate.

Materials
Pillowcase or sheet
Scissors
Thread
Needle
Armored plate pattern
9 plastic milk containers or orange juice jugs
Hole puncher

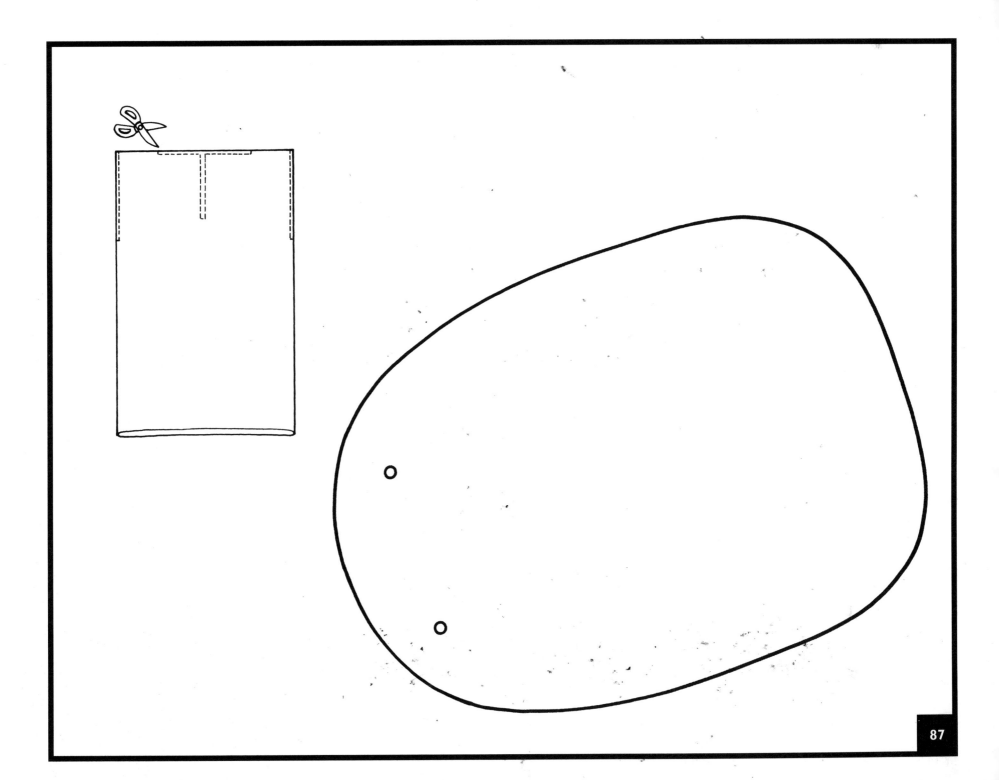

Starting at the bottom of the pillowcase, sew four plates across the bottom front. Attach the plates by sewing a stitch up through each hole and then back down through the fabric. Sew a stitch in this way several times through each hole. After the first plate is attached, sew the second plate close beside. You can use the same thread for the entire row, tying a knot of thread at the end of the bottom row.

Sew the second row of armored plates across the pillowcase so that the second row slightly overlaps the top of the bottom row. Add two more rows of armored plates until there is a total of four rows of plates. Sew one plate on the top of each shoulder.

Wear your armored tunic to protect yourself in battle.

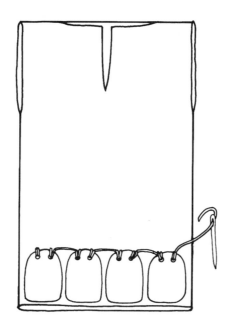 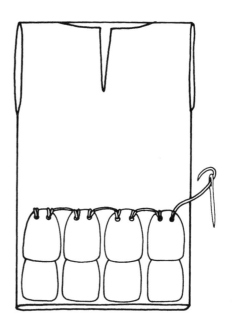

Punch two holes in the rounded edge of each piece of armor.

SETTLING DOWN

After Joshua and the Israelites settled into the Promised Land, they still fought to conquer more of the new land. Sometimes their armies moved to the north and sometimes to the south. It was easier for them to march along the Jordan Valley instead of trying to cross the mountains. One by one, some of these cities were slowly conquered, although many of the walled cities remained in the hands of the Canaanites (the people who lived in the area prior to the Israelites' arrival).

At first many of the families built their homes in the hills and settled down in the Promised Land in areas where no one else lived. But as these cities were conquered, the Israelites began moving inside the city walls.

New neighbors moved in called Philistines (say it: FILL-uh-steens) and complicated matters. The Philistines had sailed in from the Mediterranean Sea and landed along the Coastal Plain. A strong, aggressive people, the Philistines fought the Israelites for control of many of the cities.

The Israelites found that the new land was a nice place to live. After wandering around in the hot dry desert for 40 years, they were happy to settle into houses instead of tents and to plant fields of grain. They fought hard to remain in their new homes.

MAKE A FAMILY TREE

Today most boys and girls know the names of their parents, grandparents, and great grandparents. They don't really know the names of their great grandparents' parents and grandparents. Unless someone in your family studies the history about your ancestors, you probably don't know much about them.

In Old Testament days, however, it was very different. Boys and girls from Israel could trace their ancestors all the way back to Adam and Eve—the first man and woman God created to inhabit the earth. They kept long, detailed records to trace only the men in a family, as was the tradition. Occasionally, a record listed someone's mother, but only if she was a famous person or did something very meaningful.

When the Israelites arrived in the Promised Land, they knew exactly whose grandparents or great grandparents were whose. Everyone in the entire group of Israelites was related to one of the 12 sons of Jacob. (Remember Jacob? His father was Isaac and his grandfather was Abraham. Jacob is the man whose name was changed to Israel and who had 12 sons.)

After they moved into the Promised Land, the Israelites divided the land so that all the relatives of each of Jacob's sons would have their own land.

Photocopy or trace the family tree on the back of this page. Write your name on the tree trunk. Write your brothers' and sisters' names (if you have siblings) on the bushes beside the tree. Ask your parents to help you spell the names of your grandparents and great grandparents, and write these names on the lines.

To add more interest to your tree, try to find photographs where the faces of the people are as big as the apples on the tree. Cut out each person's face and glue it on the apple next to his or her name. (Check with an adult first to make sure you may cut these photographs.) If you can't cut the photographs because they're too important, use photocopies instead.

Family Tree

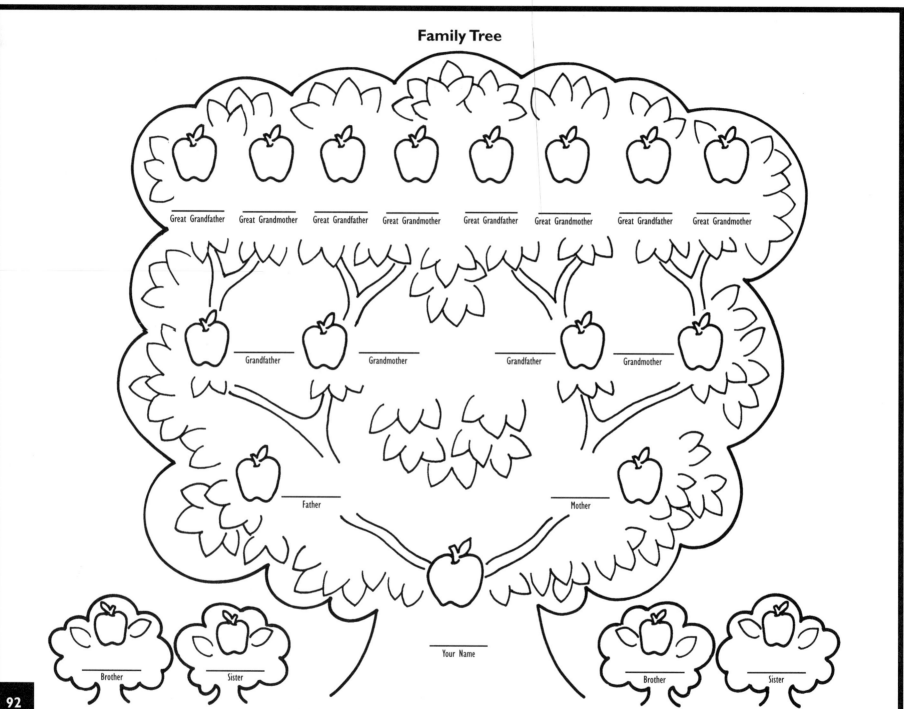

Great Grandfather

Great Grandmother

Great Grandfather

Great Grandmother

Great Grandfather

Great Grandmother

Great Grandfather

Great Grandmother

Grandfather

Grandmother

Grandfather

Grandmother

Father

Mother

Brother

Sister

Your Name

Brother

Sister

92

PUZZLE MAP

The Promised Land was divided up so that each tribe could have a part except the tribe of Levi (one of Jacob's sons). The people in the tribe of Levi were the priests and needed to take care of the Tabernacle. Since they took care of the Tabernacle, they didn't have time to farm the fields. They didn't need land to grow crops for food because all the other tribes were supposed to bring some of their food to the Tabernacle to feed the priests.

When the Israelites divided the land, they didn't give land to the tribe of Joseph either. Instead, they gave land to each half-tribe belonging to Joseph's two sons, Manasseh and Ephraim. This generosity was shown probably to make up for Joseph's brothers' having sold him into slavery.

Materials

Illustration of map

Pencil

1 sheet typing or tracing paper

Scissors

**2 9 by 11-inch
Styrofoam meat trays**

Pen

Glue

**Permanent markers,
various colors**

**Fine-tipped black
permanent marker**

Trace the picture of the map on paper, including all 12 tribal areas. This is the pattern you will use to make your puzzle. Cut around the outside edge of the paper map. Place the paper map on top of one of the Styrofoam plates and use an ink pen to trace around it. Using the pen, trace the outline of the interior sections on the paper map by lightly pressing down on the Styrofoam while tracing these interior sections. Remove the paper and mark the four subsections of the map by making deeper pen impressions. You will cut out these four sections later. Carefully cut out the outside edge of the map from the Styrofoam; try not to damage the outside edge of the Styrofoam as this will be used for the puzzle frame. When finished, you will have two pieces: the map and the map's frame.

Glue the map's frame to the other piece of Styrofoam. While this is drying, use the permanent markers to color in the different sections of the map using your pen impressions as guides to the tribal borders. Use a different color for each section. After you've colored in the sections, cut the puzzle into four pieces along the heavy pen lines drawn on the Styrofoam. Use the fine-tipped marker to label each section with the name of the tribe who settled there. Assemble the puzzle by placing the Styrofoam pieces into the frame you glued together.

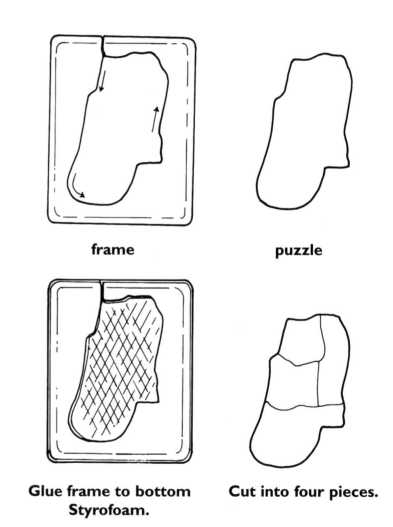

frame   **puzzle**

Glue frame to bottom Styrofoam.   **Cut into four pieces.**

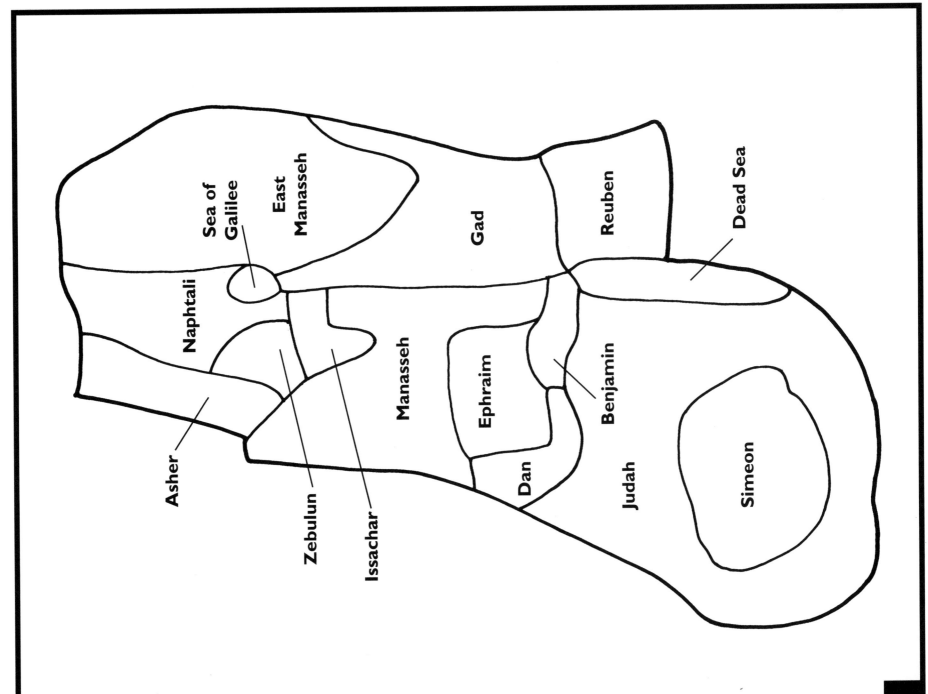

DIVISION BASED ON A CENSUS

When we look at the map of how the Promised Land was divided, it looks like it wasn't very fair. Why did some tribes get a lot of land and other tribes not very much? Why did some tribes get to live in the nice valley while others had to live in the hotter desert?

There were some very important reasons why the land was divided this way. First of all, a few years back when Moses was still alive, God told Moses to count all the families in each tribe, or take a *census*. (Say it: SEN-sis.) When Moses counted the people in each tribe, he only counted the men who were 20 years old and older. Moses ended up with a total number of 601,730 Israelites—and that didn't even include the women and children!

When Joshua became the new leader, he used the census Moses had taken. Joshua divided up the Promised Land by giving more land to the tribes that had more families. Tribes with fewer families were given smaller amounts of land.

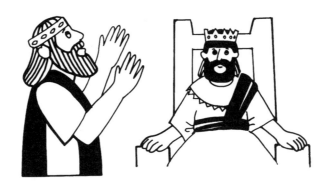

PROPHETS AND KINGS

At Home in the Promised Land

After Joshua divided up the Promised Land (Israel), the Israelites settled into villages and towns. People built their homes close together for protection. At first, small towns were built in the hills and held about 20 small houses grouped together.

Village life often centered around the farming chores and household duties necessary to survive. Children were expected to help. At home, they helped make pots, clothes, and tools for their families to use. They helped tend small flocks of sheep and goats. They helped farm the steep rocky terraces or flat steps of land carved into the hillside where they grew grapes and grains.

As the years passed, the Israelites pushed more and more Canaanites out of the land and moved down to villages built on the plains. They built homes that were very simple. Their homes were made of mud and stones. They were shaped like squares with one door, a small window, and a flat roof.

BUILD WITH HEADERS AND STRETCHERS

In the hill country, the Israelites built the walls of their homes by using mud to hold together some of the many rocks they found all over the ground. In the plains, however, they built the walls of their houses from bricks made from dried mud. To make the walls stronger, they laid the bricks together using a headers and stretchers pattern. This pattern was made by placing one long brick next to two short bricks. On the next row above, the pattern was reversed. This pattern made the wall very strong. They then covered these bricks with mud to help hold them together.

 Build a wall like one in an Israelite home, using the headers and stretchers pattern. After your wall is finished, try breaking it apart. It holds together very well. By using this pattern, the Israelites were able to build strong houses that withstood the rainy season and provided cool shade from the hot sun.

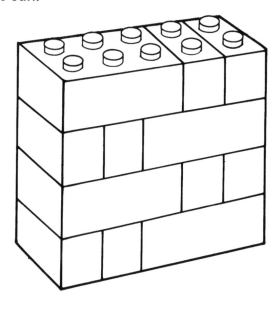

Materials

Interlocking blocks that snap together, such as Legos

AN ISRAELITE HOUSE

Houses for most families usually had one main room. This room was divided into two sections. The area around the door was a low flat floor of hard-packed dirt. Often, the fire was built in a hollow on this floor. Sometimes a tall clay oven stood over the fire. A low platform was built on the other half of the room. The family slept on the platform. Sometimes their animals slept on the dirt floor near the door.

Wealthier families often built their houses around a central courtyard. Different rooms surrounded the courtyard. These rooms were used for sleeping, storing food supplies, and for animal stables. The family usually cooked their meals over a fire in the courtyard.

Can you imagine living in a small house with only one room and sharing it with the animals? It's no wonder that the Israelites spent much of their time at home sitting on their rooftops. The roof was often used like a room. The Israelites dried fruit and grain on the roof. They visited with their friends on the roof. On hot summer nights, the families slept on the roof to try to stay cool. A short wall was built all around the edge of the roof so the people wouldn't fall off.

The roofs were made from branches placed across wooden beams and covered with mud. They often needed to be repaired after a heavy rain. Also, grass usually grew on top of the roof from seeds in the mud. Families kept a heavy roller on the roof to roll back and forth to flatten the floor. This helped flatten the grass and fix the leaky cracks.

Because their homes were close to the fields and they often carried their food in baskets and placed it on top of the roof, people often had mice, snakes, and insects in their homes searching for food. If there were cracks in the mud brick walls, snakes might hide there for a shady nap away from the hot sun. Mice would scurry up the walls and steal grain from the baskets on the roof. Insects could be found anywhere in the house.

As well as having a very simple house, the Israelites only used very basic furniture. They slept on animal skins, which they unrolled at night. They used small clay oil lamps to help them see inside the dark, dusky room. They stored most of their food in clay pots and jars. They cooked their meals over a fire or baked bread in a simple oven, and they ate while sitting around an animal skin spread out on the floor for a table.

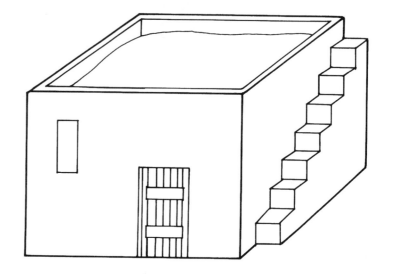

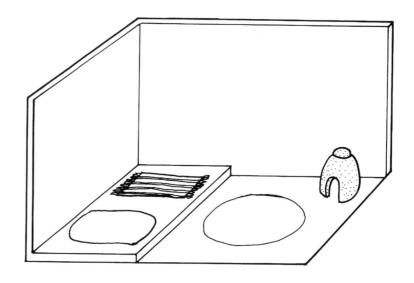

The Israelites lived in simple houses with basic furniture.

LIGHT UP A LAMP

The house of an Israelite was often a very dark place. The Israelites used oil lamps to help them see when they were inside. The oil lamp looked like a clay dish with one edge that was pinched together. A rag or twisted piece of string was set in the dish so that one edge lay on the pinched edge. This end was lit. As the piece of rag burned on one end, the other end soaked up the oil in the dish. Such an oil lamp could usually burn for two or three hours before more oil was needed.

 (Adult supervision required for fire safety.) Form a fist-sized lump of clay into a shallow bowl. Shape and pinch the clay in one area so that it is the highest part of the bowl's edge, forming a lip. Use your finger or a pencil to make a groove in this lip.

Bake this clay lamp as directed on the clay package. Allow to cool.

Materials

Oven-bake clay

Pencil

Olive oil or vegetable oil

Cotton string

Scissors

Fireproof surface such as a cookie sheet

Matches

Pour ¼ inch of olive oil into the lamp. Cut a three-or four-inch length of cotton string and put it completely in the oil. Pull out one end of the wet string and lay it over the pinched edge of the lamp. Keep the other end of the string in the oil.

Place the lamp on a fireproof surface such as a cookie sheet. Ask an adult to light the end of the string with a match. Watch carefully how the lamp burns. Is there a lot of smoke? (The pinched end of the clay lamp might turn black. Make sure it doesn't catch on fire.) Blow out the flame when you are finished using the lamp.

Imagine using this lamp as your only light in the house. How would you have to change your activities (for example, household chores) if this were true?

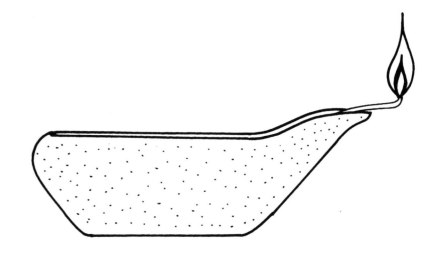

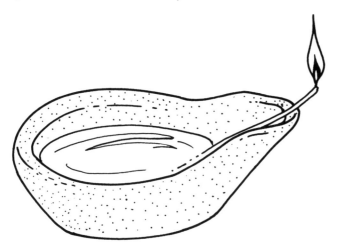

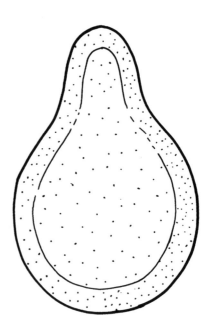

top view of lamp

KEEPING CLEAN

Washing clothes and keeping clean were important ways to help prevent diseases. However, keeping clean wasn't easy! The Israelite houses didn't have bathrooms. They didn't even have water in their houses!

To take a bath, people often washed in a nearby stream or river using a soap made from plant ashes mixed with fat. If they wanted to wash themselves at home, they had to first get water from the well in the middle of the village. They poured water into jars and carried them home. They let the jars of water sit in the sun all day if they wanted to bathe with warm water. Then they poured the water into a large bowl. Since the bowl was too small to use as a bathtub, they washed themselves as we wash our faces and hands at a sink. Only very rich people had bathtubs.

After the people washed, they rubbed olive oil into their skin. This helped their skin stay healthy and also protected them from insect bites by forming a protective coat over their skin. Rich people perfumed the olive oil that they rubbed on themselves or mixed in herbs such as rosemary or marjoram.

Toothbrushes hadn't been invented yet. To help keep their breath clean, people often chewed on herbs that had a mint flavor.

How did the Israelites go to the bathroom? They either went outside and used a field or they used buckets, which were then emptied into ditches along the streets.

Materials

Jar of water

Large mixing bowl or pot

Olive oil

Peppermint candy

Try washing as the Israelite children did! Set a jar of water out in the sun during the day. When the water is warm, pour it into a large bowl or pot. Wash your face and hands as best as you can. Then rub a tiny amount of olive oil into your skin. To freshen your breath, eat a piece of peppermint candy.

FOOT WASHING

Since many people went barefoot or wore sandals, their feet got really dirty. If your friends walked to your house to visit you, it was considered good manners for you to wash their feet! In fact, if you didn't wash their feet, or have a servant wash their feet, it was seen as an insult or very bad manners.

Invite your friends to your house and wash their feet when they arrive! Have one person sit down in a chair and take off her shoes. Pour the water from the jar into the bowl. Wash your guest's feet carefully and then dry them with a towel. Then wash the next person's feet. Imagine doing this every time your friends came over to play!

Materials

Chair

Jar of water

Large mixing bowl or shallow dishpan

Towel

WASHING CLOTHES

The Israelites often made soap from mixing olive oil with ashes from plants that had soda in them. Dirty clothes were taken to a nearby stream. The soft paste of soap was rubbed into the clothes. As they rubbed the clothes in their hands, the running water from the stream helped wash the dirt out.

In the cup, mix two spoonfuls of baking soda with two spoonfuls of olive oil. Kneeling at a bathtub or standing at a sink, rub this soapy paste into the dirty socks. Turn on the water and let it wash over the socks as you rub them. How clean do your socks get?

Materials
Cup
Spoon
Baking soda
Olive oil
Dirty pair of socks

TIME FOR DINNER

Living in the Promised Land, the Israelite families prepared their food from the crops they grew and the animals they kept. Other food was made from the plants, animals, and insects that were found throughout the land. Grains such as wheat, corn, and barley were commonly grown. These grains were baked into flat breads by pressing circles of dough against the side of a tall oven. Or, the grains were roasted on a flat pan over the fire. Sometimes, the grains were even eaten raw.

Most people ate very little meat; only wealthier people could afford this food. Usually, children and their families ate meals of bread, fruit, vegetables, nuts, cheese, and olives. Beans and lentils were often eaten and fruits such as figs and grapes were plentiful. Olives, onions, garlic, and salt were used to season the meals.

Milk from sheep and goats was made into yogurt, butter, or cheese.

The Israelites didn't have much of a choice when they were thirsty. They drank milk, water, fruit juice, or wine. Milk came from the family goats. Water was pulled out of the village well. Juice was made from fresh grapes. Wine was also made from grapes and was a common drink because it could be stored in containers of animal skins and kept for a long time.

To make the wine, the Israelites grew grapes in their vineyards. They picked the ripe grapes and carried them in baskets to a large stone pit called a *winepress*. To press the grapes and squeeze out the juice, the men walked around in the winepress in their bare feet. They squished the grapes between their toes! The grape juice ran out into a smaller pit where it was left for at least six weeks to turn into wine.

107

DESIGN A BEE BASKET

Honey and dried fruit were used to sweeten cakes and other desserts. Often, people simply dipped bread into honey for a tasty treat. Israelite families hung baskets near their houses, hoping bees would build a hive in the baskets and supply them with honey.

(Adult help suggested.)

Cut the plastic bottle in half as shown. The bottom half can be a little shorter than the top. Cut a one-inch-wide rectangle out of the bottom half of the bottom and cut a one-inch square from the top half so that when the two pieces are fitted together, there is a one-inch opening for the bees to enter.

Push the bottom half of the bottle up so that it is slightly inside the top half of the bottle. Add glue to secure the two pieces together. Glue a piece of burlap around the bottle, cutting a hole over the

Materials

1 plastic liter bottle (for large bee basket) or 1 individual-sized plastic water bottle (for small bee basket)

Scissors

Glue

Burlap

Household string

opening. To fit the burlap around the top of the bottle, cut slits in the burlap and glue these strips of fabric around the bottle opening.

Tie a string around the neck of the bottle and hang it outside from a branch of a tree far from any doorway to your home. Once it is hung, *never* get up close to your bee basket to investigate whether it's being used; only look at it from a safe distance.

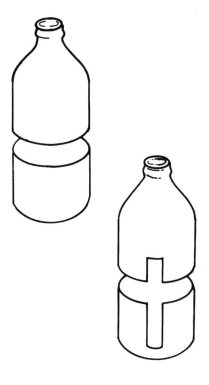

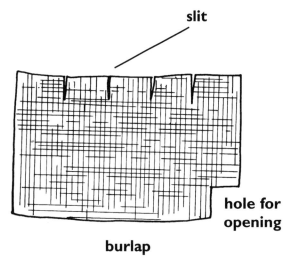

slit

hole for opening

burlap

JUDGES, PROPHETS, AND KINGS

Moses led the Israelites out of Egypt. After he died, Joshua became the new leader. Joshua led the Israelites into the Promised Land. After the people lived in the new land for many years and built houses and villages, Joshua died.

The people needed someone to take Joshua's place. They needed someone who made sure the people in the villages didn't steal from each other or break any other laws. They needed someone who could organize an army if the Philistines from neighboring villages attacked them.

After Joshua died, the *elders*, or oldest people, in each village settled arguments and made sure the village laws were upheld. These elders met at the gates of their villages and discussed problems in the villages and decided what to do about the laws.

Along with these elders in each village, there were tribal chiefs, or leaders, of each of the 12 tribes. Also, any person who people believed was picked by God was considered a leader. These leaders were known as *judges*. One judge was a woman named Deborah. The Israelites agreed that God had picked her to lead them during this time because she possessed great wisdom. She also communicated with God. Deborah held her court of judgment under a palm tree. People from nearby villages came to her with their problems and arguments. Deborah judged who was right and who was wrong.

The judges sometimes led small groups of Israelites into battle against their neighbors who had stolen crops and food from them or wronged them in some other way.

These judges were also often known as prophets. (Say it: PRAW-fets.) A *prophet* was a person who spoke to God. The prophets passed messages from God to the people. Samuel was such a prophet.

During Samuel's lifetime, the Israelites began asking for a king. They were tired of having their laws decided by the village elders and tribal chiefs or by people who were chosen as judges. Sometimes the judges couldn't get a big army ready in time for battle. Sometimes the tribal chiefs couldn't agree on how to solve big problems. The Israelites thought that if they had a king, they would always have an army ready to protect them. A king would rule over the entire country and make important decisions for everyone. The people asked Samuel for a king.

The first king of Israel was chosen. His name was Saul. (Say it: it rhymes with ball.) King Saul organized the Israelites into an army and fought against the Philistines. King Saul died in a battle against these enemies. After he died, David became the second king of Israel in 1011 B.C.

HIDING IN CAVES

King David fought many battles even before he became king. Often, out in the hillsides of the country, David and his soldiers hid from their enemies in caves. There were many caves throughout the country. David and his men could make the caves larger by digging with their tools. They carved seats out of the stone wall of the cave and carved shelves to put oil lamps on. Usually, David and his men stayed near the opening of the cave where there was more light. Food, weapons, and supplies were stored at the back of the cave.

Being a soldier often meant camping out in a cave. To experience what army life was often like for David and his men, build your own cave by spreading blankets or sheets over a card table or desk. Crawl underneath the blankets and spend time in your cave. Is it easy to see? Is it uncomfortable? Imagine planning important battles while hiding in your cave.

Materials
Small desk or card table
Blankets or sheets

hiding inside a cave

MAKE A LYRE

David learned to play various instruments while he was a boy and continued his love of music as he grew up and eventually became the king of Israel. One of King David's favorite instruments to play was the *lyre* (say it: Lie-er). The lyre was a small harp. It could have many different shapes. When David was a young boy, he carried his lyre to the fields and played it while he was watching his father's sheep. As he grew older, he visited the palace to play soft music for King Saul. As king, David still played the lyre and wrote songs that praised God.

To make the lyre, wrap the rubber bands along the length of the hanger, spacing them evenly apart. To play the lyre, strum along the length of the rubber-band strings. Try plucking the strings to make the sounds of different notes. Write a simple song and try singing with the notes you can make on your lyre.

Materials

10 small, sturdy rubber bands

Plastic hanger

MAKE A SISTRUM

The sistrum was a percussion instrument with a handle. Rings and bars hung on a metal frame that was attached to the handle. A person held the handle and shook the sistrum back and forth to make a metallic ringing sound. David probably shook a sistrum in his hand while he danced to praise and worship God.

Wash and dry a milk carton, opening the top completely to form a box. Fold the top of the milk carton down inside the box. Press firmly in place.

Punch two holes on the sides of the carton, opposite each other and close to the bottom. Insert the dowel rod through the holes as shown and tape to the back of the box.

Use a hole puncher to make two sets of holes opposite each other and toward the top of the

Materials

1 individual-sized milk carton

Hole puncher

½ inch dowel rod, 12 inches long

Duct tape

Scissors

Needle-nose pliers

16-gauge Rebar tie wire (available at hardware stores) or flexible craft wire

Metal washers, 1 inch diameter

carton on the sides of the carton without the dowel. Cut two 5-inch lengths of wire. Thread one wire through one hole and put six washers on the wire and then thread it through the opposite hole. Make a loop and twist the wire so it cannot go back through the hole. Use the pliers bend the wire up over the top of the carton and back inside. Add the other wire and washers in a similar manner.

When finished, shake the sistrum to create a lively beat.

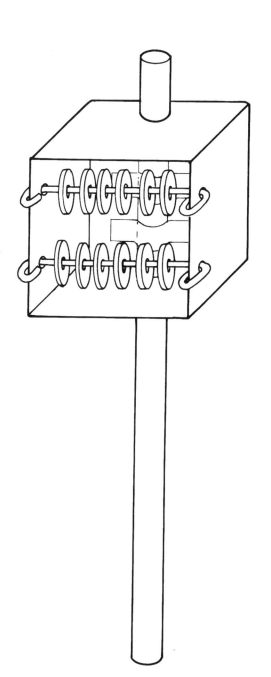

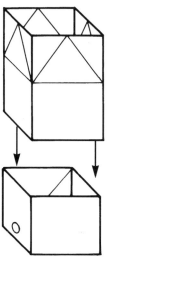

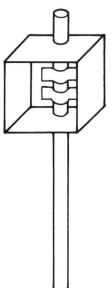

MAKE A TIMBREL

The timbrel was similar to a modern-day tambourine. The Israelites made a timbrel by stretching an animal skin over a hoop. The hoop was then decorated around the edge with bells. When David was king, he wrote many songs calling for the people to shake their timbrels and dance with joy because they loved the God of Israel.

To make your timbrel, use 8-inch lengths of narrow ribbon to tie the jingle bells evenly spaced around the outer edge of the larger (outer) embroidery hoop. Tie the ribbon so the bells stay on the outside edge of the hoop. Also try to position the knots from the ribbon on the outside edge.

After the bells are tied on, stretch the piece of fabric over the inner embroidery hoop and place the outer hoop with the tied-on bells over the fabric.

Tighten the hoops together. Trim the extra fabric away from the bottom of the hoop. Now grab your timbrel and dance, using it like a tambourine!

Materials

¹/₄-inch-wide fabric ribbon

Scissors

6 small jingle bells

1 10-inch wooden embroidery hoop

¹/₂ yard knit fabric

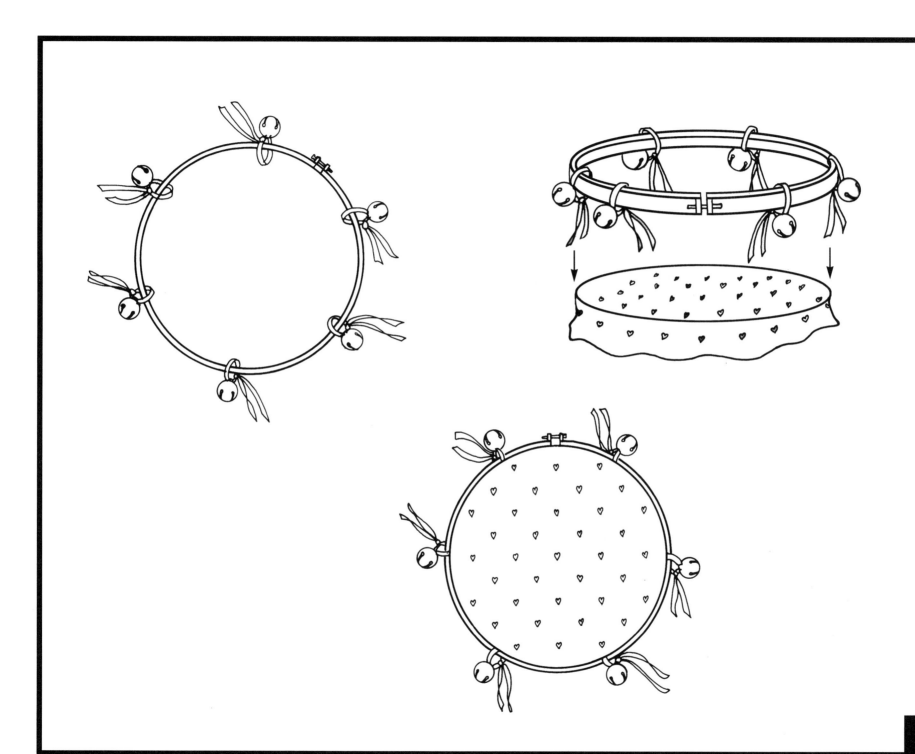

MAKE CYMBALS

When the musicians wanted to make loud, joyful noises for the entire gathering of people to hear, they held two large metal cymbals in their hands and clashed them together. Everyone in the village heard the cymbals when they were played.

Materials

2 flat metal lids from saucepans

 Hold the two lids, one in each hand. Clash them loudly together.

FIGHTING THE ENEMY

There were many different groups of people who lived near the Israelites. As king, it was David's job to help protect the Israelites from the people who tried to hurt them.

The Philistines lived on the western side of the Israelites. Their armies were known for their tall, strong warriors. The Philistines tried to keep the Israelites from making weapons of iron, because iron weapons were stronger than stones or clubs.

The Midianites lived on the southern side of the Israelites. Their armies were known for appearing out of nowhere and making surprise attacks. Riding in from the desert on their camels, the Midianites stole the Israelites' food, grain, and animals.

The Assyrians lived on the northern side of the Israelites. Their armies stole the Israelites' riches. The Assyrians used these riches to build their own beautiful temples and palaces.

The Babylonians lived on the eastern side of the Israelites. When their army showed up, they often took most of the people away as prisoners. The Israelites lived as slaves in other cities. Only very poor, older, and weaker Israelites were left behind in their homes.

You can see that having a king meant a lot to the Israelites. A king could organize a better army to protect them from their enemies. A king could get the money needed to feed the soldiers and make the weapons.

DIFFERENT WAYS TO FIGHT

The Israelite army used different ways to fight their enemies. Sometimes they surprised their enemies with an ambush. An *ambush* was when the army would hide and wait for a good time to attack. The Israelites might hide in the fields outside a city. When a group of men from the city came out to the fields to harvest or check on their livestock, the Israelites would ambush them in surprise.

Sometimes the Israelites surrounded a city that had thick, sturdy walls protecting it. Their army simply waited outside the city. The people of the city might throw stones or shoot arrows at the soldiers. If the army was strong enough, these defensive tactics wouldn't hurt them too badly. Soon the people in the city would run out of food or water because they couldn't leave the city to tend their fields or flocks. After a while the people would surrender or were too weak to fight back when the Israelites broke down the city walls.

Sometimes the Israelite army faced the entire army of an enemy. Sometimes each army would select its best soldier to fight the best soldier of the opposing army. Whichever soldier won the individual conflict determined which army won the whole battle.

A SLING AND SOME STONES

Before David was king, he visited the Israelite army to deliver food supplies to his brothers who were soldiers in the army. At the time, the Israelite army was fighting the Philistine army. Instead of having a full-scale battle, though, the Philistines had chosen their best soldier, Goliath. Goliath wanted to fight one of the Israelite soldiers in a one-to-one battle to decide which army would win. All the Israelite soldiers felt too scared to fight Goliath. He was too tall and too big and looked too strong! But David wasn't afraid. He took the sling he used as a shepherd to throw rocks at bears and lions. He picked up several small stones from the ground. He threw one stone at Goliath's forehead and knocked him down dead! The Israelites won the battle!

You can make a sling like the one David used in battle.

Materials

Illustration of sling

Scissors

2 by 4-inch piece felt

Shoestring or thick yarn

Cotton ball, large

Pebble

Use the pattern to cut a small piece of felt for the sling. Cut two horizontal slits in the felt, one on each of the shorter sides. Cut a shoestring in half or use two 15-inch lengths of thick yarn. Thread one string through each slit and knot.

If using the sling indoors, use a cotton ball. Only use a pebble if you are outside away from people and buildings. Place the cotton ball in the felt pocket of the sling. Hold both strings in your hand. Twirl the sling and let go of one of the strings. The cotton ball should shoot out.

David practiced many hours with his sling to learn how to aim and hit a target. You can practice, too.

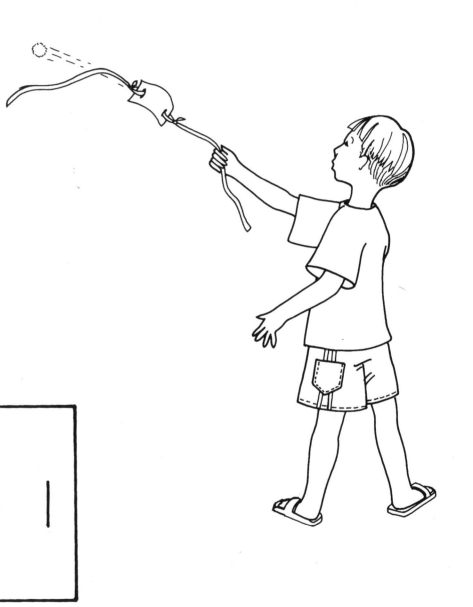

A BOW AND A QUIVER OF ARROWS

A common weapon soldiers used was a bow with arrows. The bow was made from wood. The arrows were made from reeds, or sturdy grasses, that had sharp metal-like points. The soldiers carried their arrows in quivers strapped across their backs. A quiver held about 30 arrows. This activity shows you how to make a bow just like the ones used in the Old Testament days.

To Make the Bow

(Adult help required for safety.)

Ask an adult to help you make the bow. Use the shears to cut a 28-inch-long stick. Trim off small branches. Using the shears cut a groove near each end of the stick as shown, being careful not to break it.

Materials
Sturdy clippers or shears
Ruler
1 28-inch stick that is roughly $^{3}/_{4}$ inch in diameter (the stick shouldn't be brittle or it will break)
Household string
Scissors
Pencil eraser (the kind that fits on top of a pencil)
1 $^{1}/_{4}$-inch dowel rod, 18 inches long
Glue
Craft knife
1 2-liter plastic soda bottle
1 old pair of men's large socks

123

Test the stick by bending it to see how long the bowstring should be to create a good tension on the bow without breaking it. A 28-inch stick will probably use a 22-inch bowstring. (Allow a couple inches for making a loop at each end of the string.) Tie an overhand knot with a 1-inch loop at one end of the string. Make a loose loop at the other end of the string.

String the bow as shown, pressing gently but firmly on the center of the stick. (Don't bend it too hard as it might break.) Put the loop around the other end of the stick and tighten the knot.

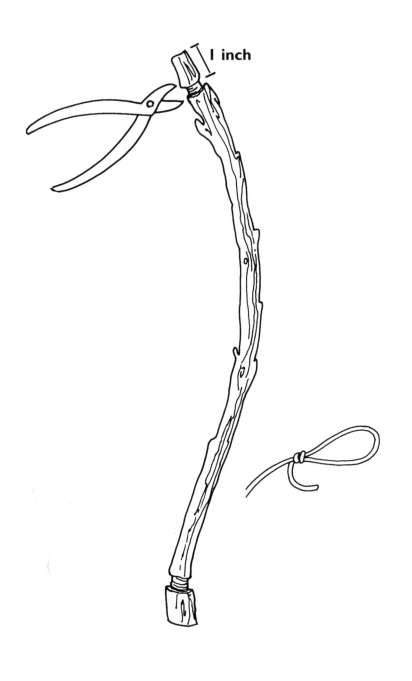

To Make the Arrows

 Glue the pencil eraser to one end of the dowel rod to be the point of the arrow.

cut off top here

stop here

cut here

Open the sock out flat.

To Make the Quiver

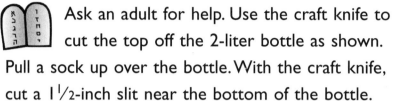 Ask an adult for help. Use the craft knife to cut the top off the 2-liter bottle as shown. Pull a sock up over the bottle. With the craft knife, cut a 1½-inch slit near the bottom of the bottle. Cut through both the sock and the bottle at once.

To make the strap, cut along both edges of the other sock. Do not cut across the toe. Open the sock out flat. Insert one end of the strap into the slit on the bottle. Pull the strap up through the bottle and out at the top. Tie a knot.

Put your arrow in the quiver. The Israelite soldiers usually carried 30 arrows in their quivers. Wear the quiver strapped over your shoulder.

David often practiced shooting arrows with his friend, Jonathan. To practice with your friend, too, take your bow, arrow, and quiver out to a playground or large field away from people and buildings. Set a target on the ground, such as a large rock. Take turns shooting arrows to try to hit the target.

THE SHIELD

Since there were no guns at this time, soldiers often fought each other up close. They needed shields to protect themselves. A regular shield was a piece of wood covered with leather. Soldiers usually wore the shield on a strap on their left arm.

Cut a large circle out of the cardboard, at least 9 inches in diameter. Cut a strap for the shield from a piece of cardboard. For a 9-inch shield, you will need a 3 by 12-inch strap.

Ask an adult to help you use the hole puncher to poke two holes at each end of the strap. Place the strap across the back of the shield. Use a pencil to

Materials

Pencil

Ruler

Cardboard

Scissors

Hole puncher

Brads or pipe cleaners

Felt, brown or gray

Craft glue

make marks through the holes onto the back of the shield. Use the hole puncher to punch these holes out. Use brads (or pipe cleaners) to attach the strap onto the shield.

To finish the front of the shield, cut a design from felt and glue the pieces of felt onto the front. Press firmly in place and allow to dry.

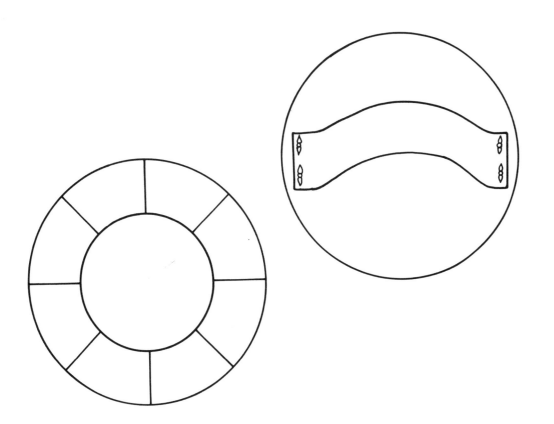

Wear the shield on your left arm as soldiers did back then.

KING SOLOMON'S TEMPLE

After King David grew old and died, his son Solomon became the third king of Israel. The years Solomon ruled were some of the wealthiest and most glorious years the people of Israel ever knew.

King Solomon built the Temple in Jerusalem. The Temple was very similar to the Tabernacle that Moses built. There was one big difference, though. The Tabernacle was a tent. The Temple was a beautiful building made of gold! According to today's prices, about $36 billion worth of gold was used to build the Temple. Expensive silver, special wood, and sturdy stone were also used.

With such a valuable building inside the city, the wall around Jerusalem helped protect the Temple's gold from being stolen by robbers from neighboring non-Israelite cities. It took seven years to build the Temple, and it became known as one of the most wonderful buildings in the world.

The Temple was known as the house of God. It wasn't built to hold a lot of people, so it was small. Only the priests were allowed to go inside. The people, however, were encouraged to visit the courtyard to worship God and make sacrifices.

Inside the Temple, it was usually dark. There were only a few small windows near the top. Plus, there were candles. It was totally dark in the room in the back called the Most Holy Place where the Ark of the Covenant was kept.

Solomon's Temple had a stone altar for making sacrifices. It had a large bronze basin for the priests to wash before they went into the Temple. There were golden candlesticks, the incense altar, the Ark of the Covenant, and the table that held

12 loaves of bread. This was all very similar to the furniture used in the Tabernacle built by Moses. Rooms were built along the sides of the temple to hold offerings and supplies.

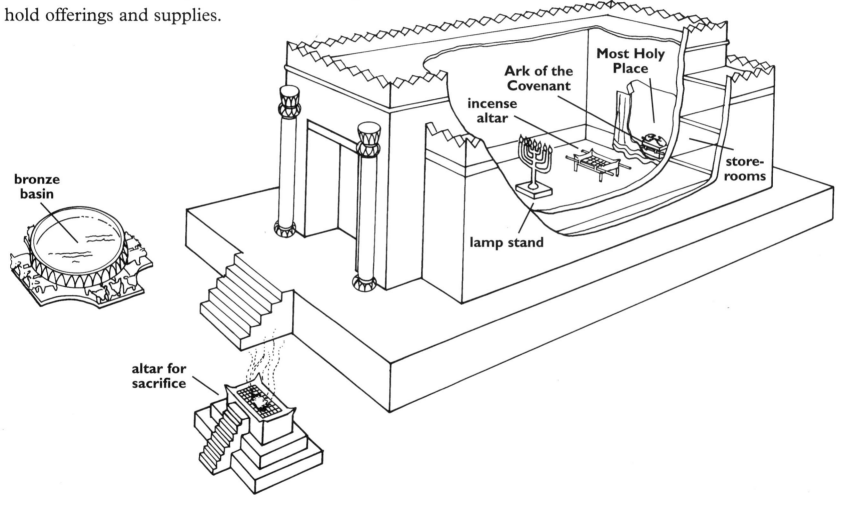

bronze basin

Ark of the Covenant

Most Holy Place

incense altar

store-rooms

lamp stand

altar for sacrifice

King Solomon's Temple

CLOTHING WORN BY KING SOLOMON AND HIS WIVES

Not only did King Solomon have a lot of money and build a lot of buildings, but he also married a lot of women. He had more than seven hundred wives! Many of his wives were given to him as gifts from the kings of other countries.

Solomon was very wealthy, so he and his wives wore expensive clothes that were very beautiful. Solomon's wives wore long flowing tunics and robes made from finely woven fabric. Their head coverings were also pretty pieces of fabric that covered their hair. They wore costly jewelry, such as bracelets, anklets, earrings, and necklaces, made of gold and silver.

Solomon's tunics and robes were also made of expensive fabrics. He wore a crown to show he

queens' outfits

king's outfits

was king. One of the crowns he probably wore looked like a fancy turban covered with pearls and valuable gems. Solomon also had special outfits of armor made to wear in battle.

People were very busy during the years King Solomon ruled. Ships were built to carry gold and other valuable things. King Solomon's Highway was an important road where traders traveled back and forth to carry spices and building supplies to and from other countries. Farmers were busy growing crops to feed all of Solomon's wives and children. People were forced to pay heavy taxes to pay for all of King Solomon's expensive projects such as erecting buildings.

MAKE A MEASURING TAPE

To help keep track of everything, the Israelites measured things differently from how we do today. A short distance was measured in how far someone could shoot an arrow. A longer distance was measured in how far a group of donkeys could walk in one day.

To measure the length of an object, people used their own bodies. A finger was the main unit of measurement. (It was $1/2$ inch long.) Four fingers made a hand. (This was 3 inches.) Three hands made one span. (This was 9 inches.) Two spans made one cubit. (This was about 18 inches.)

To make your own measuring tape that compares inches to the way the Israelites measured things, use the illustration as a guide. Mark off inches along one side of the ribbon and fingers along the other side of the ribbon. (Both marks should be on the front of the ribbon. Experiment first on a short piece of ribbon to see whether permanent marker or ink pen writes best.) Tape the ribbon next to the illustration to help hold the ribbon in place as you mark off the measurements.

Materials

Illustration of measurement

60 inches 1-inch-wide fabric ribbon

Fine-tipped permanent marker

Ink pen

Scissors

Clear tape

When your measuring tape is finished, hang it on the wall with the bottom on the floor. Stand next to it and measure your height. How many spans tall are you? How many fingers? How many inches?

Take the measuring tape off the wall and use it to measure other objects.

(Option: you can make the tape out of strips of paper instead of a ribbon.)

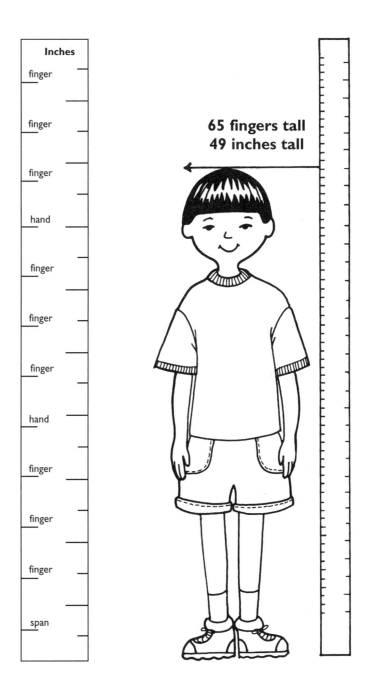

65 fingers tall
49 inches tall

MAKE A SCALE

Traders often weighed spices, silver, or other objects to see how valuable they really were. Things were weighed on simple balanced scales. The object was placed on one side of the scale. Special stones were placed on the other side of the scale. These stones were often marked according to how much they weighed.

Often, people tried to cheat by saying their stones weighed different amounts than they actually did. Traders usually carried their own set of stones in their pockets to use on scales so that they could be sure of an accurate weight.

Materials

Stick or hanger

Household string

Scissors

2 matching paper cups or plastic containers

Hole puncher

If using a stick, tie a loop of string around the center of the stick so that it balances. Use this loop to hang the stick from a doorknob or, if using a hanger, hook the hanger neck over a doorknob.

Punch three holes evenly spaced around the top of each cup. Cut six lengths of string, which are at least 12 inches long. Lace one string through each cup hole and knot the string. Gather the three secured strings and tie the ends around one end of the stick or hanger. Do this on the other end, too, being careful that both cups hang the same distance from the end and to the same level.

To weigh an object, place the object in one cup. Place small stones in the other cup until both cups balance evenly. Count the number of stones you used. Are the most valuable things you weigh always the heaviest?

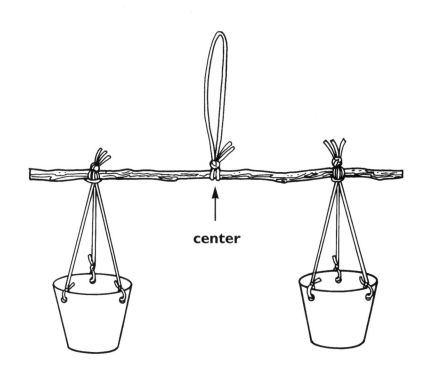

center

FAR AWAY FROM HOME

New Kings for Israel

After King Solomon died, other kings ruled the land. Most of these kings, however, weren't very fair rulers who cared about the welfare of the common people. They cheated poor people and took their money. They murdered innocent people. They didn't pray to God. After awhile, all the people in Israel started following the kings' bad examples, too. Many years went by. Prophets spoke to the people in Israel. The prophets told the people that if they didn't start changing their ways and doing good deeds, they would be punished. Most people simply ignored the prophets. They kept lying, stealing, and cheating.

Finally, a king from another nation marched into Israel. King Nebuchadnezzar (say it: NEB-uh-cud-NEZ-er) from Babylon captured Jerusalem and all the other Israelite cities. His armies destroyed the beautiful golden Temple built by King Solomon.

Some people escaped and ran to Egypt. But King Nebuchadnezzar's armies captured thousands of Israelites. He forced them to march far, far away and live in different countries. He forced many of them to be slaves in his kingdom.

Only poor people were left behind to live in Israel to farm the land. Children and adults from wealthier families were taken to live in Babylon (say it: BAB-e-lon). A young man named Daniel was among the crowd of people forced to live in Babylon. Because Daniel and his friends were intelligent and handsome, they were chosen to undergo three years of special training so they would be able to serve King Nebuchadnezzar. Daniel and his friends were given new names. They were schooled and taught to become valuable members of the king's palace.

CHOOSING A NEW NAME

Names were very important to the Israelites. Their names had special meanings. Their names described their personalities or told about their family. Sometimes their names described the type of riches or wealth they would have in the future. But when the Israelites were forced to go to the new land and serve King Nebuchadnezzar, he changed everyone's name to Babylonian names! The Israelites hated this.

Here is a list of girls' and boys' names that were commonly used in Israel. (Some of these names have more than one meaning.) Try choosing a new name for yourself from this list that tells something special about who you are.

Girls' Names
Abigail means "father's joy."
Beth means "life."
Esther means "salvation."
Eve means "giver of life."
Deborah means "busy."
Hannah means "full of grace."
Naomi means "beautiful."
Rachel means "motherly."
Rebecca means "peacemaker."
Ruth means "friend."
Sarah means "princess."

Boys' Names
Aaron means "teacher."
Abraham means "exalted father."
Adam means "the man."
Benjamin means "certainly or surely."
Daniel means "a judge."
David means "beloved."
Eli means "faithful."
Isaac means "he laughed."
Jacob means "favored."
Jeremiah means "exalted."
Jesse means "strong."
Joshua means "God saves."
Nathaniel means "God given."

LETTERS FROM THE NEW LIFE

Letters and documents from the time of Nebuchadnezzar have been found by archaeologists; some were written by Israelites who ran away to Egypt, and others were written by Israelites who lived as captives in different countries. These letters and documents were sometimes stored in clay jars, which kept them safe for centuries.

These letters and documents tell us a lot about what life was like for the Israelites when they lived far away from home. Many of the children as well as their parents began to like the cities they were originally forced to live in. They found jobs and built homes and grew content in their new life.

Read through the following letter. What does it reveal about what life was like for Israelites who lived in a different country from the Promised Land?

My name is Noah. I am from the tribe of Benjamin. I am living in the land of the Pharaoh. It has been many months since King Nebuchadnezzar marched in from the north and destroyed my city in the land of my fathers. My family and I were fortunate, though. We escaped the sword and ran away to the south where we now live with the Egyptians.

I now grow dates to sell in the marketplace. The money I earn from the dates has been helpful. I was able to rent a small piece of land by the river. I built a home here for my wife and my son and my three daughters. I want to state right now that when I become too old to farm the dates anymore, my son Ishmael gets the house and may rent the land to grow dates for his business. Until that time, he will help me grow the dates.

The people here are fair to us. They do not cheat us, but pay a full price for our dates. They let us practice our own faith even though it is very different from theirs. Even though my wife and I miss the city of our own country, we will live here and not go back. Life is good for us here.

REMEMBERING THE LAWS

The Israelites who lived far away from home worried that their children would grow up and not know about their faith in God. They worried that the children wouldn't learn their history about how Moses had led them to the Promised Land.

The people wanted to teach their children about their faith and help everyone remember the important laws Moses had written for them to follow. Not everyone knew how to read and write. *Scribes* were people who learned how to read and write. Scribes started writing down the laws. Then these laws were read aloud at large gatherings so that everyone else could hear them. This taught the children and helped the older people remember what they had learned long ago in their homeland.

Some of the laws may sound funny to us today. Today we have different farming methods and different machines from what the Israelites had many thousands of years ago. Their laws were written to help them stay healthy and grow good crops with the farming methods and machines that they had. These laws made sense to them.

Here are some of their laws. As you read these, try to figure out why these laws were important to the Israelites.

Laws

1. Don't plant your field with two different kinds of seeds (Lev. 19:19).
2. Don't wear clothes made of two different kinds of material (Lev. 19:19).
3. Sound the shofar everywhere on the tenth day of the seventh month (Lev. 25:9).

4. If a slave hides at your house to escape from slavery, don't send him back to his master (Deut. 23:15).

5. Don't charge your brother interest or make him pay extra money if you lend money to him (Deut. 23:19).

6. Don't cut the hair on the sides of your head or clip off the edges of your beard (Lev. 19:27).

7. If aliens live in your neighborhood, treat them with kindness (Lev. 19:33).

8. Every seven years, don't plant your fields or prune your bushes (Leviticus 25:3,4).

9. If a man just got married, he's not allowed to fight in the army (Deut. 24:5).

10. Every 50 years, everyone is supposed to move back and live in the same house as their grandparents. All property is restored to its original owner (Lev. 25:10,13).

11. When you pick grapes, only pick the field once. Don't pick it twice (Lev. 19:10).

12. Always use an honest ephah and hin [standard weights] when measuring things (Lev. 19:36).

Here are some of the reasons each of these laws was written. They are numbered to correspond to the numbers of the laws.

1. People who worshiped idols might have mixed different kinds of seeds together when they planted their fields. The Israelites wanted to be different from these people.

2. People who worshiped idols might have woven different kinds of material together for a religious reason. The Israelites wanted to stay away from any type of activity that would make people think they worshiped idols, too.

3. There was a special holiday on this day that began the Year of Jubilee, which occured every 50 years. During this year, people who had sold their land if they were poor were able to get their land back. Slaves were also

set free. By blowing the shofar everywhere, people would be reminded that it was a holiday. They didn't have televisions or radios to remind them of important dates.

4. This law was made to encourage people to help each other.

5. This law was made so the rich couldn't get even richer by lending money to people in their family.

6. Egyptians cut their beard and hair in certain ways to worship their gods. The Israelites didn't want to look like they were worshiping Egyptian idols.

7. Aliens weren't people from outer space! An alien was a word used to describe a stranger. This law commanded people to be kind to strangers.

8. Farmers didn't have fertilizers or chemicals to add to the ground as we do today. By not planting any crops every once in a while, it gave the ground a rest. This way the ground stayed healthy for growing good crops.

9. With this law, a king couldn't order a newly-wed husband off to war. This gave a little bit of protection to couples who just got married so that they could have a family.

10. It was very important to the Israelites that each person's land stayed in the family. Often, people might become poor and lose their land to pay back money they owed. By making this law, people would always be able to get their land back after 50 years.

This was supposed to help so there wouldn't be very many poor people.

11. Again, this was a law to help the poor people. The farmers were only supposed to pick grapes once. After that, the poor people could come into the fields and pick the grapes left over. This was true for all crops.

12. When people sold things, they measured them on balancing scales. Some people cheated by putting something too heavy or too light on the other side of the scale. An ephah and hin were standard weights used for measuring liquids or dry goods. This law was made so people could not cheat each other.

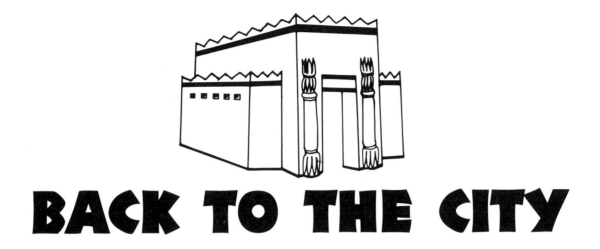

BACK TO THE CITY

After King Nebuchadnezzar died, the empire in Babylonia grew very weak. Finally, Cyrus, the King of Persia, captured the city of Babylon in 539 B.C. and made this part of the Persian empire. King Cyrus brought many changes to his new empire. Some of these changes were very important to the Israelites. The most important change of all was that King Cyrus told the Israelites they could move back to their homes. King Cyrus even told the Israelites they had his approval to rebuild the Temple in Jerusalem!

MAKE THE CYRUS CYLINDER

Archaeologists found a large clay cylinder (say it: SILL-in-der). This cylinder is shaped like a log and is called the Cyrus Cylinder. There is writing on the cylinder that tells how Cyrus captured the great city of Babylon and how he let all the captive people move back to their homes.

Pretend you are writing a list of important details that you want other people to know, as if you are writing a proclamation like that appearing on the Cyrus Cylinder. You can make a list of the chores you completed around the house and then present it to a parent, or you can describe an award you won for schoolwork completed or volunteer work you contributed to the community.

> I, Cyrus, King of Persia, have captured the great city of Babylon.
> In Babylon, I found many people from other countries.
> I gathered these people together and returned them to their homes.
> Whoever wanted to leave was able to leave Babylon and go back to their homeland.
> I gave my approval for them to return to Jerusalem and rebuild their Temple.

Leave space at top and bottom for glueing.

the Cyrus Cylinder

Materials

4½ by 6-inch piece paper

Scissors

Pen or pencil

Cardboard tube from a
toilet paper roll

Glue

Clear tape

Write this list on the piece of paper and glue it to the cardboard tube. Place a piece of tape on the edges if necessary.

As you work, imagine how happy the Israelites felt when they heard the news announced on the Cyrus Cylinder. After having lived in captivity for many years, they were finally allowed to return to their homes.

I, Amanda, Queen of my bedroom, have cleaned my room, picked up all my toys, and straightened my books...

CREATE YOUR OWN SEAL

Whenever a king wanted to show everyone that he gave his approval for something, he used his special seal. A *seal* was a baked piece of hard clay or a carved piece of stone. It had a special design on it that told the person's name. Often, the seal was put on a ring or worn as a necklace. When something was written in clay, such as the Cyrus Cylinder, the person who was writing pressed his seal into the clay to show everyone that it was official. Today people sign papers with their signature, but back in Old Testament days people stamped the clay with their seals.

Sometimes special seals were designed to use on pots or objects made from clay. Seals have been found stamped on clay jars that say which city they were made in. Jars and pots that were made in Jerusalem were stamped with a seal that said "Jerusalem" or "The City."

Materials

Oven-bake clay

Pointed toothpicks

(Adult help suggested.)

To make a seal, flatten a piece of clay that is about the size of a quarter. Use a toothpick to write your name or the name of your city into the clay. Write the letters backward so when you stamp the seal on something, they will appear in the correct order. Add a design around the word, if you want.

Bake the seal in the oven, according to the directions on the package. Allow it to cool.

Try making a small pot or jar out of the clay. Carefully press your hard clay seal into the bottom of the pot or jar. Then bake it in the oven according to the clay package directions.

RETURNING TO JERUSALEM

Several different groups of people traveled back home to Jerusalem. Taking a trip of this length wasn't easy! People didn't have cars, trains, buses, or planes to travel in. Most of the time, everyone walked. Even the small children had to walk. If they brought animals along, the camels and donkeys could be ridden or used to carry loads. Cows could pull wagons.

Long trips were dangerous, too, because groups of bandits hid along the dirt roads. It was important for people to travel together in a large group so that they could help protect themselves from attack.

The first group of Israelites to return home were very eager to live again in their hometowns and rebuild the Temple. They had to carry everything they owned back to Israel. Also, they had to take back a lot of the supplies they needed to build the Temple. It took a lot of camels and donkeys to carry everything on their trip! One list says that 42,360 Israelites; 7,337 servants; 200 singers; 736 horses; 245 mules; 435 camels; and 6,720 donkeys returned on this trip. They brought back more than 5,000 gold and silver containers that had been stolen from the Temple. These containers had been stolen by King Nebuchadnezzar and brought to his palace to use. But now King Cyrus wrote a law stating that the Israelites could take the Temple furnishings back home to Jerusalem where they belonged. When this group of people returned to their homeland, they immediately began rebuilding the Temple. Later, another group returned to Jerusalem. They continued working on the Temple and rebuilding parts of Jerusalem that had been destroyed by King Nebuchadnezzar. It took many years to rebuild the Temple. When it was finally done, though, some of the people were sad. The new Temple wasn't as beautiful or as big as the one King Solomon had built many, many years before.

A few years later, there was a new Persian king whose name was King Artaxerxes (say it: are-tax-IRKS-ees). This king gave an Israelite priest named Ezra permission to move back home, and he also gave a lot of political power to Ezra. King Artaxerxes wrote a special letter for Ezra to show everyone. The king let anyone who wanted to move back home with Ezra. The king even gave Ezra a large number of gold and silver coins so that he could purchase things that were needed in the Temple! When Ezra returned to Jerusalem he brought more than 5,000 men with him. It took more than four months for them to walk home.

DESIGNING COINS

During Old Testament days, coins told a great deal of information about the history of the different countries. Poor countries used copper or bronze to make coins. Wealthy countries used gold or silver.

Every time a new king ruled the land, new coins were made with a picture of the king's head on them. Also, the coins were stamped with a number that told how much they weighed. Heavier coins had more gold or silver in them and were worth a lot more money.

Jerusalem became part of the Persian empire after King Cyrus had captured Babylon. Even after King Cyrus died, Jerusalem stayed part of the Persian empire for many years under different Persian kings.

A lot of coins in the Persian empire had a picture of an owl on one side. This showed that the coins were from Persia. When Ezra received gold and silver coins from the king, he was probably given some coins that were designed with the picture of an owl on them.

gold coins

coin from Persia

REBUILDING THE WALL

King Artaxerxes later gave permission for an Israelite named Nehemiah to go back to Jerusalem. Nehemiah had asked the king for permission to return home and rebuild the city of Jerusalem. His request was granted. When Nehemiah returned to his homeland, he was appointed governor of the city. As he examined the ruined city, he realized how important it was that the city of Jerusalem be completely surrounded by a large wall. This would protect the city from other armies, which might try to attack the city again.

Nehemiah organized many different people to help rebuild the wall completely around the city of Jerusalem. But it wasn't an easy project.

It was expensive to get the materials to rebuild such a large wall. There were also a lot of people in Jerusalem who didn't like these strangers moving into their city and changing things. When the Israelites had been forced to leave Jerusalem 70 years ago, King Nebuchadnezzar moved other families in. The new families didn't want all these groups of Israelites to keep coming back!

Nehemiah had to give all the builders weapons to carry in case someone attacked them while they were building the wall. It was very dangerous work. But finally, after only 52 days, the wall of Jerusalem was rebuilt. The city was again safe from attack.

MAKE A PLUMB LINE

It was very important to build a straight, sturdy wall around the city of Jerusalem. After the wall was built, horses would ride around the top of it and people would march on it.

The Israelites didn't have fancy tools like those we have today. Their tools were simple ones. Hammers were made of wood. Saws were simple cutting tools. To help make sure the walls were straight, they used a plumb line. A *plumb line* was simply a heavy weight tied onto the end of a string. When the string was held beside the wall and the weight hung down at the bottom, the string was perfectly straight. The builders compared the wall with the straight string and adjusted the wall until it was straight, too.

Materials

3-foot-long piece of string

Weight, such as a large metal washer or a rock

 Tie the weight carefully to one end of a piece of string. Hold the other end of the string in your hand and let the weight hang freely. Don't let the weight touch the ground. Hold the string still until the weight stops swinging back and forth. The string should now be perfectly straight up and down.

Hold your plumb line next to a doorway or next
to a wall. Is the door straight? Is the wall straight?
See how many straight things and how many crooked
things you can find.

MAKE LOTS AND USE THEM

After the wall was built around the city of Jerusalem, Nehemiah met with the people to decide who would actually live inside the city. Even though it seemed like the safest place to live, life inside the city wasn't always easy. Not as many people lived in the city as had lived there before. A lot of the homes were burned or falling apart. People who lived inside the city couldn't be farmers and grow crops as easily as someone who lived in the country outside the city walls. It was important, though, for as many Israelites as possible to move into the city of Jerusalem if they wanted their homeland to belong again to the Israelites instead of to the strangers King Nebuchadnezzar had moved there many years ago when he destroyed the city.

A decision needed to be made about who would live inside the city and who would live on the land out farther in the country. As the governor of Jerusalem, Nehemiah counted all the Israelites in Jerusalem and in the nearby villages. Then he and his friends threw special dice known as "lots" to decide who would come and live in Jerusalem. Out of every 10 families, 1 was chosen to live inside the city walls. The other non-Israelites remained in the city.

To the Israelites, using lots wasn't at all like gambling. They believed that God would decide which lot was supposed to be chosen. Any time they had a question that they wanted to answer fairly, they used lots.

Historians aren't really sure how the lots were used by the Israelites. Sometimes small pieces of marked wood were placed in a jar with a small opening. The jar was filled with water. After someone shook the jar around to mix up the pieces of wood inside, the jar would be tipped over to let one piece of wood fall out. The person whose name was written on the piece of wood would be the one who was chosen.

Other times, small pieces of marked wood were put into a jar or basket with a wide opening. Someone simply reached inside the jar or basket and picked one of the pieces of wood with the name of a person who was then chosen.

Sometimes lots might have been used in the same way we use dice today. A person would shake the lots in his hand and throw them out on the ground. Whichever side they landed on determined the decision.

When you are with a group of your friends, write your names on lots and choose one lot to see who goes first in a game. Have each person write his or her name on one side of a plastic cap and decorate the other side with a sticker. Place all the caps in a basket or jar. Close your eyes and choose one of the caps. The person whose name is picked goes first.

Materials

Caps from plastic milk containers or orange juice jugs

Small stickers to fit on caps

Pens or permanent markers

Basket or wide-mouthed jar

choosing lots

CALCULATE TITHES

After the wall around Jerusalem was finished, Ezra and Nehemiah met with all the Israelites. They had a great celebration and a long feast to rejoice that their beloved Jerusalem was again their safe city.

Ezra was a scribe who knew how to read and write. He read the laws of Moses aloud to the people so that they could learn what was important to their faith.

Nehemiah made sure that the people took care of the city of Jerusalem and the Temple. It took a lot of work and a lot of money to keep everything working well. And just as the laws from Moses' time had required, Nehemiah had everyone bring to the Temple 10 percent of the food they grew or the money they earned. This was known as the people's *tithes* (say it: It almost rhymes with size).

To calculate how much tithe you would be expected to bring every year to the Temple, add up your allowance for an entire year. Divide this number by 10. That is the amount of money you would be expected to pay every year to help keep the Temple working well and in good repair.

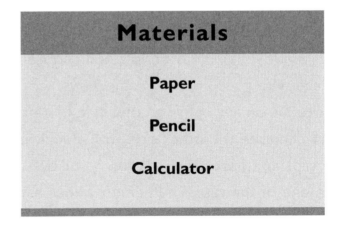

Materials

Paper

Pencil

Calculator

You can also calculate how much tithe you might pay each month. Just add up your allowance for one month. Divide this number by 10. That is the amount of money you would be expected to pay to the Temple every month.

Many times, people living in Old Testament days didn't have money. They had sheep or baskets of dates or jugs of olive oil. Nehemiah expected them to count all the animals they had or crops they grew each year. They were supposed to bring 10 percent of their flocks or their crops to the Temple as their tithe.

Allowance for May

$1.50 each week
x 4 weeks
$6.00

$$10 \overline{)6.00} = .60$$

60¢ tithe
for 1 month

THE CITY

After the walls of Jerusalem were rebuilt, it was safe for people to live there. Over the years, Jerusalem became an important city once again.

Housing was built for the priests and the servants who worked in the Temple. People moved into sections of the city that had been destroyed or burned. They rebuilt new homes and lived there. Shops were built for jewelers, potters, and other businesses. Many businesses were built just outside the city wall as well.

The Persian government kept the road to Jerusalem in fairly good condition. Soldiers and men on horses acted as police and protected large groups of traders traveling to the city. The Persian empire had plenty of ships to sail to other countries. Wonderful things from these other countries found their way to the city of Jerusalem. If you were growing up in Jerusalem, you could walk to the markets and buy spices and perfume from Arabia, beautiful pottery and jewelry from Greece, and metal tools and weapons from Egypt!

There were many people in Jerusalem who made crafts to trade for all these things. Jerusalem became a busy, exciting place to live. It was an important city once again.

MAKE A SPICE CHART

Herbs and spices were very important to people during Old Testament days. They were used to keep food from rotting and to make food taste better. They were mixed with oils and used to help keep people clean. They were used for medicine. They were even used to prepare a dead person's body for burial.

Large groups of travelers on camels and donkeys took spices from Jerusalem to other countries. These groups were called *caravans* (say it: CARE-uh-vans). Caravans also brought different spices from other countries back to Jerusalem. People bought and sold the spices at the market in the city.

Many spices that were used a lot during Old Testament days are still being used today. Garlic was used to make bread taste good. Herbs such as cumin, dill, mint, coriander, cinnamon, and saffron were used in cooking, too.

Materials

Scissors

Poster board or cardboard

Ruler

Pencil

Markers or pens

Glue

Variety of spices

Cut the poster board into a 12-inch square or a large enough piece for the number of spices you are using. Draw a grid on the poster board as shown in the illustration. Draw one space for each spice. Label each space with the name of a spice. Put a spot of glue in each space and sprinkle the spice on the glue so that it sticks and completely covers the glue. Decorate the chart as you like. Once the glue dries, hang up your chart and take time to smell each spice. Imagine how good the spices smelled at the markets in Jerusalem!

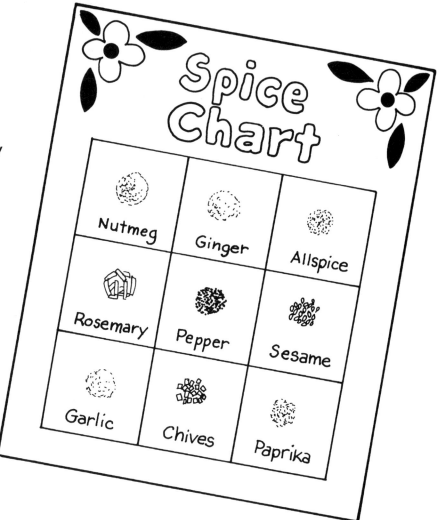

PLAY MARKET DAY

The sun was hot at the market in Jerusalem. People often sat under fabric shades to sell their wares.

 Set up several card tables and cover them with blankets or sheets to look like the shelters people used in Jerusalem.

If you're with a group of friends and want to set up a large area to look like the market in Jerusalem, you can make more shelters by draping sheets over chairs. Set up something different to sell at each shelter. Put as many things as you can in baskets for your customers to see.

Let half your friends each sit under a shelter and pretend to sell their items. These people should have scales to measure out their items and small rocks to balance the scales.

Materials

Card tables or small desk and chairs

Sheets and blankets

Baskets or large containers

Variety of items that might be found in a Jerusalem market, such as:
- **Food (spices, fruit, bread, fish)**
- **Clothes (fabric, yarn, sandals)**
- **Animals (toy farm animals or stuffed animals)**

Scale from page 134–135 and rocks to use as weights

Coins, such as pennies and nickels

The rest of your friends can walk from one person to the next, choosing what to buy. They can use coins to pay each person when they buy something. But don't just pay the people their asking price. The market in Jerusalem was a noisy, crowded place. Nothing had a price tag on it. People asked how much something cost and the seller told them the price. They often argued back and forth as they weighed everything out until finally both were satisfied with the price. Usually, there was a lot of shouting, too!

Have fun pretending you're at the market in Jerusalem! Smell the spices. Listen to the noises from the animals. Hear all the shouting and arguing! See all the happy faces of people who buy wonderful things from countries far, far away.

at the marketplace

LIFE IN THE OLD CITY

The city of Jerusalem became a busy, busy place after the wall was built again. The wall was wide enough for people to go on top of it and march or ride their horses. The houses were often so close together that people could walk from rooftop to rooftop throughout the city. And of course, the Temple was the most important place for the Israelites to visit.

Jerusalem was an important city and a busy place during Old Testament days, and it still is today. Archaeologists have discovered many clues about Old Testament days from studying the ancient buildings found in Jerusalem. Today, archaeologists continue their search for clues by digging up some of the area around the city. Many people travel to Jerusalem today to visit and to find out more about the past. A city filled with excitement, Jerusalem offers great adventures to people who live there or travel there to enjoy the wonders of its history.

BIBLIOGRAPHY

Abram, Elise Sherman. "Archaeological Analysis: Pieces of the Past." 1996. www.rom.on.ca/digs/munsell/. (7 June 1998).

Alexander, David, and Pat Alexander. *Eerdmans' Concise Bible Handbook*. Minneapolis, MN: Lion Publishing, 1973.

Backhouse, Robert. *The Student Guide to Bible People*. Minneapolis, MN: Augsburg, 1996.

Beers, Gilbert V. *Big Book of Bible Learning*. Sisters, OR: Gold 'n' Honey Books, 1995.

Black, Naomi. *Celebration: The Book of Jewish Festivals*. Middle Village, NY: Jonathan David Publishers, Inc., 1989.

Blankenbaker, Frances. *What the Bible Is All About for Young Explorers*. Ventura, CA: Regal Books, 1986.

Cansdale, George. *All the Animals of the Bible Lands*. Grand Rapids, MI: Zondervan Publishing House, 1970.

"Egypt, Ancient." In *Compton's Encyclopedia*. Volume 7. Chicago: Compton's Learning Company, 1992.

Daiches, David. *Moses: The Man and His Vision*. New York: Praeger Publishers, 1975.

Dowley, Tim. *The Student Bible Guide*. Minneapolis, MN: Augsburg, 1996.

Downey, David, Frederick Eiselen, and Edwin Lewis. The *Abingdon Bible Commentary*. New York: Abingdon-Cokesbury Press, 1929.

"First Names." 1999. www.xxxeros.com/firstnames/girlsj-z.htm. (11 February 1999).

Geis, Darlene. *Let's Travel in the Holy Land*. Chicago: Children's Press, Inc., 1965.

Godwin, Johnnie and Roy Edgemon, editors-in-chief. *Disciple's Study Bible: New International Version*. Nashville, TN: Holman Bible Publishers, 1988.

Gower, Ralph. *The New Manners and Customs of Bible Times*. Chicago: Moody Press, 1987.

Halley, Henry. *Pocket Bible Handbook*. Chicago: Henry H. Halley, 1944.

Hertzberg, Arthur. *Judaism: The Classic Introduction to One of the Great Religions of the Modern World*. New York: Simon & Schuster, 1991.

Inter-Key Inc. "Parenting." www.parentzone.com/parents/bnames.htm. (11 February 1999).

Irwin, C. H. *Irwin's Bible Commentary*. Philadelphia, PA: Universal Book and Bible House, 1928.

Keyes, Nelson. *Story of the Bible World in Map, Word, and Picture*. Pleasantville, NY: The Reader's Digest Association, 1962.

Kushner, Harold. *To Life! A Celebration of Jewish Being and Thinking*. Boston: Little, Brown and Company, 1993.

MacArthur, John. *The MacArthur Study Bible*. Nashville, TN: Word Publishing, 1997.

Matthews, Victor. *Manners and Customs in the Bible*. Peabody, MA: Hendrickson Publishers, 1991.

North, Archer. "Ancient and Beautiful Biblical Names for Baby." 1999. www.fortunecity.com/lavendar/chelmsford/9/bubnames.html. (11 February 1999).

Raphael, Chaim. *Festival Days: A History of Jewish Celebrations*. New York: Grove Weidenfeld, 1990.

Rose, David, and Gill Rose. *Passover*. Austin, TX: Raintree Steck-Vaughn, 1997.

Rosmorduc, Serge. "A Short Introduction to Hieroglyphs: Sign grouping." 1995. http://webperso.iut.univ-paris8.fr/~rosmord/Intro/Intro.html. (7 June 1998).

Smith, William. *A Dictionary of the Bible*. Grand Rapids, MI: Zondervan Publishing House, 1970.

Walton, Fiona. *Let's Explore Inside the Bible*. Minneapolis, MN: Augsburg, 1994.

Water, Mark. *The Children's Encyclopedia of Bible Times*. Grand Rapids, MI: Zondervan Publishing House, 1995.

Wigoder, Geoffrey, ed. *Illustrated Dictionary and Concordance of the Bible*. Jerusalem, Israel: G. G. The Jerusalem Publishing House Ltd., 1986.